CERTAIN NOCTURNAL DISTURBANCES

GHOST HUNTING BEFORE THE VICTORIANS

CERTAIN NOCTURNAL DISTURBANCES

GHOST HUNTING BEFORE THE VICTORIANS

BY

TIM PRASIL

BROM B🎃NES BOOKS

The front cover illustration is "Nunnery of Mannel or Emauel," drawn by Francis Grose. It appears in his *The Antiquities of Scotland,* vol. 2 (Printed for Hooper and Wigstead, 1797) between pp. 66-67. The back cover illustration is "Athenodorus Confronts the Spectre," drawn by Henry Justice Ford. It appears in Leonora Blanche Lang's *The Strange Story Book* (Longman's, Green, and Co., 1913) p. 81.

ISBN-10: 1-948084-11-2
ISBN-13: 978-1-948084-11-6

It is the same with all those that are called accredited ghost stories usually told at the fireside. They want evidence. . . . I may mention, as one of the class of tales I mean, that of the late Earl St. Vincent, who watched, with a friend, it is said, a whole night, in order to detect the cause of certain nocturnal disturbances which took place in a certain mansion.

—Sir Walter Scott, 1830

CONTENTS

INTRODUCTION

Before the Victorians

The Victorian era began in 1837 and ended in 1901, the years that Queen Victoria ruled what was then called the United Kingdom of Great Britain and Ireland. In this time and in this place, the question of why *ghosts* have tantalized and baffled humanity across the globe for millennia garnered serious, scholarly attention. Among those voices calling for such study was Catherine Crowe, who gathered a wide variety of reports about supernatural and occult experiences, then organized them into a surprisingly popular book titled *The Night Side of Nature; Or, Ghosts and Ghost Seers* (1848). Meanwhile, around 1850, a number of Cambridge University students began to meet with the intention of examining reports of hauntings. Apparently, not much came of the project, but it inspired the more formal Ghost Club, founded in 1862—and this led to the Society for Psychical Research, founded in 1882. The latter two organizations still exist today, and neither has confined its focus to only ghosts. Along with mesmerism, clairvoyance, and similar topics, both groups were especially motivated to validate or debunk the phenomena occurring at Spiritualist séances.

Consider, too, the contribution the Victorians made to the literary ghost-story tradition with writers such as Charles Dickens (1812-1870), Sheridan Le Fanu (1814-1873), Charlotte Riddell (1832-1906), and Edith Nesbit (1858-1924). It's little wonder, then, that in the early 2000s, we envision the ectoplasm of ghosts swirling with the fog of Ripper-era London and sense something charming—yet slightly chilling—in those cornices, cupulas, and other ornate flourishes of houses built during the 1800s. One might reasonably conclude that *ghost hunting* started in the Victorian era.

But there's a substantial history to this noble quest that predates the Victorians. In fact, the term *ghost hunt* and its derivations *ghost hunting* and *ghost hunter(s)* appear in pre-1837 publications with some regularity. The longer I look, the farther back in time I go, but so far one of the earliest uses I've unearthed is in Elizabeth Gunning's 1794 novel, *The Packet*. There, a character named Sir William Montreville interviews people who claim to have seen a specter at the local church. Though he's skeptical, Sir William joins with his servant to form what Gunning calls a "ghost-hunting party." Late at night, the duo patiently hide in one of the pews at the haunted site to conduct some nocturnal surveillance, the time-honored practice of ghost hunters. Other documents that use the term include 1804 newspaper and magazine articles about that year's Hammersmith Ghost case (covered in Chapter Seven of this book), an 1808 play, an 1817 book about premature burial, and an 1820 family history.[1] Remember that the term *ghost hunt* was quite likely spoken before written. Figure in any documents using it that have been lost or that remain untouched on dusty library shelves or in decaying trunks. With this in mind, I suspect various forms of ghost hunting were fairly well known with that label in Britain for about four or five decades before the Victorians.

Ghost hunting *teams* have a history that reaches back even further. They certainly looked differently than how we see them today on television, YouTube, and elsewhere, but Chapter Four addresses how assembling a committee to investigate claims of ghostly phenomena dates back at least to 1534. That's the year Francis I, King of France, appointed a group—a mix of clergy and lay people—to investigate claims that a church graveyard in Orleans was haunted. One of the most famous paranormal investigative teams was assembled in 1762, when a ghost was purported to be visiting Cock Lane in London. I discuss this in Chapter Four. All along, ghost hunters have had to position their work against those who insisted that phenomena being misinterpreted as *supernatural* or *paranormal* were, in actuality, entirely *natural* and pretty darned *normal*. Indeed, as we'll see, many important ghost hunters were among those seeking to debunk a haunting. It's misguided to assume that "everyone back then believed in ghosts," a sweeping generalization often aimed at people in some vague part of the past. An example of this appeared in 1863, when George Cruikshank described people of a century-and-a-half earlier this way: "The gullibility of the public was much greater at that time than now, and they would swallow anything in the shape of a ghost." As discussed in Chapter Three, Joseph Glanvill (1636-1680) was carefully *debating* such things about the time Cruikshank indicates. Even Pliny the Younger—a man born when years had only two digits and who died when they had three[2]—retold the story of a ghost hunt to someone he knew might think it questionable, if not complete baloney. (This ancient investigation is discussed in Chapter One.) In other words, debates about whether or not ghosts are real seem to be almost as old as recorded encounters with them. It is as if disagreement is embedded into the DNA of humanity.

The opposition faced by those working to prove the existence of ghosts leads to the need for sound, convincing evidence. A conscious pursuit of exactly that also comes before the Victorians. The above-mentioned Glanvill was an investigator who strongly believed in interaction between the supernatural and natural realms, but who also valued reliable, firsthand testimony supporting the reality of that interaction. We'll see that he applied this method to his investigation of a case commonly called "The Drummer of Tedworth."

Even the notion of the purposeless ghost—a ghost with no clear mission for manifesting and no special message to convey—appears *prior* to the 1800s. This has been presented by some ghostlore scholars as something unique to the nineteenth-century.[3] However, in Chapter Five, I make the case that the Hinton Ampner haunting of the late 1760s features exactly this kind of phenomena despite various attempts to make the haunting fit the traditional pattern of a ghost returning to, say, guide the living to a hidden deed or to serve as observable evidence of the cursed existence following a sinful life.

In a nutshell, then, ghost hunting—its key methods, its main challenges, even the term itself—all predate the Victorian era.

Defining "Ghost Hunter"

Of course, all of this talk about pre-Victorian ghost hunting depends on clarification of who exactly constitutes a *ghost hunter*. The definition used in this book involves individuals who fit the following criteria:

1) Ghost hunters are not themselves the haunted party. Rather, they learn of a stranger's alleged haunting, travel to it, and make the necessary arrangements to investigate. A slight exception here is John Jervis. He investigated weird phenomena at Hinton Ampner, his sister's haunted manor. He didn't permanently reside there, but unlike most of the other ghost hunters I'll discuss, he was related to the residents. If this compromised his objectivity in any way, it might have been counterbalanced by his co-investigators, John Bolton and James Luttrell.

2) While some of the ghost hunters to be discussed have a clear bias for or against the possibility of spirits crossing between the dimensions, they all are open-minded enough to bother investigating a

situation in which such a crossing is suspected. Belief in ghosts might best be understood as existing on a sliding scale. Those on the far ends are so convinced, so rigid, they probably wouldn't bother confirming their convictions or risk having them challenged. The ghost hunters in this book might lean one way or the other—but they do so from somewhere in the middle of that scale.

3) They apply the basic, time-tested strategies of paranormal investigation. This often means interrogating witnesses and/or closely examining the site by listening to how sound travels through walls, vents, or chimneys; looking for evidence of rodents or similar animals; checking the pipes, etc. Almost always, it involves those overnight stakeouts that I call nocturnal surveillance.

My hope is that each of the historical figures I present reflects more than a glimmer of how ghost hunting is understood and conducted now in the early 21st century. Indeed, tracking the evolution of ghost hunting across the centuries might stir feelings of connection between ghost hunters still living and their very long, very fascinating heritage.

Getting All My Ghosts in a Row

The organization of this book is *not quite* chronological. First, it's divided by "Legendary Ghost Hunts" and "Historical Ghost Hunts." This might be slightly confusing, since the legends are historical and some might say the history is infused with legend, too. For the purpose of this book, the key difference is the legends are cases that had been shared orally for several decades before being put to paper. In other words, there is no reliable documentation of the events *from the time* to suggest those events actually happened. Parson Ruddle's handling of a case often referred to as "The Botathen Ghost" is the most troublesome here, but I address those problems in Chapter Two.

The second section, then, features hauntings and investigations that were documented in writing close to when the events were happening. These cases *are* presented chronologically.

In most chapters, I open by carefully following the original sources to narrate a case's ghostly manifestations and the investigation of them. However, I do so in my own words while sometimes modernizing the language in quotations, which I also do throughout the book. The idea, of course, is to make these stories more easily accessible to my readers without the distractions of archaic punctuation, capitalization, etc. After presenting each case, I offer an analysis of it. This will focus on some recurring element of ghostlore—for example, bones substantiating a haunting—and/or how the investigation illustrates a facet of ghost hunting that is still relevant today—for example, the desire to find reliable evidence.

Despite my efforts to create order, I often found myself entranced by some element of a case and driven to explore that topic before returning to the main thread. It was very much like wandering through a haunted mansion and stepping into a room filled with, say, ghosts of headless horses. I felt compelled to have a closer look at those horses before returning to the hallway. (I'm still stymied by what their necks look like: bloody stumps? carefully sutured? smoothly congealed?) In this regard, this book might read a bit like my own ghost hunt through the long history of ghost hunting. Almost any exploration of history is, in a sense, a ghost hunt and vice versa.

This expedition will take us to several haunted houses, a haunted moor, a haunted field, a haunted neighborhood, and one sadly *unhaunted* burial vault. At first, the specters we'll encounter are more folklore than fact. The later ones, though, are well documented. Some turn out to be hoaxes. All of them are *centuries* old. However, I don't think that the advanced age of these hauntings makes them any less important and intriguing than more recent ones. You might even find them a bit *more* so.

And I hope you'll discover the same about those who bravely and carefully investigated these old hauntings. They are the pillars of the ghost hunting tradition.

---

[1] Elizabeth Gunning, *The Packet: A Novel,* vol. 4 (Printed for J. Bell, 1794) p. 5. Regarding the Hammersmith case, see "Melancholy Accident," *True Briton,* January 6, 1804, p. 4, and "Domestic Incidents," *Universal Magazine* 1 (January 1804) p. 63. The play is D. Lawler's *The School for Daughters* (Printed for the author by R. Juigné, 1808) p. 50. The books are John Snart's *Thesaurus of Horror: Or, The Charnel House Explored!!!* (Sherwood, Neely, Jones, 1817) p. 166, and Henry Nugent Bell's *The Huntington Peerage* (Printed for Baldwin, Cradock, and Joy, 1820) p. 251.

[2] George Cruikshank, *A Discovery Concerning Ghosts; With a Rap at the "Spirit Rappers"* (Frederick Arnold, 1863) p. 6. The actual dates of Pliny's birth and death are circa 61 CE and circa 113 CE respectively.

[3] See Andrew Lang, *Cock Lane and Common-Sense* (Longmans, Green, and Co., 1894) p. 95, and R.C. Finucane, *Ghosts: Appearances of the Dead & Cultural Transformation* (Prometheus, 1996) pp. 194-204.

PART ONE

LEGENDARY
GHOST HUNTS

CHAPTER ONE

PHILOSOPHERS IN
HAUNTED HOUSES

At first, the two philosophers discussed in this chapter might seem as if they should be dealt with separately, given when and where they lived. In the first century BCE, Athenodorus was born in Tarsus, a location now in Turkey. He traveled to Rome and spent a good part of his life there. On the other hand, Antoinette du Ligier de la Garde Deshoulières was born in 1638—seventeen centuries later— in Paris, France. In 1694, she died in the same city. In terms of chronology and geography, then, they are certainly an odd pair.

In terms of ghost hunting, though, Athenodorus and Deshoulières have significant similarities. First, the investigations led by both were recorded so long after their deaths that it's probably better to file their stories under "Legend" or even "Parable" rather than "Verified History." The source of the earlier chronicle is a letter written by Pliny the Younger (c. 61 CE – c. 113 CE), who lived roughly a century after Athenodorus. Deshoulières' probe into a haunted room popped up in various books and magazines in the early 1800s, about two centuries after she had lived. In other words, it's entirely possible neither historical figure ever *really* went on a ghost hunt. They're only *reputed* to have done so in the way that, for instance, young George Washington is fabled to have been unable to tell a lie about chopping down a cherry tree.

Another similarity between Athenodorus and Deshoulières is in how their respective narratives work to prompt readers to rethink their fear and conceptions of ghosts. Pliny recounts the long-gone investigator's inquiry into a haunted house while asking his original reader if such supernatural situations are possible, and the narrative illustrates how a ghost, though spooky looking, might be more a victim than a villain. The anecdote about Deshoulières warns against being quick to assume a mysterious visitation must surely be supernatural when, with a bit of daring and level-headedness, it's easily explained as completely natural.

Speaking of courage and calm, the two philosophers' cases also illustrate the qualities that make a successful ghost hunter. Even if largely fictionalized, the ghost hunts of Athenodorus and Deshoulières dramatize how walking bravely into a place alleged to be infested by a sinister spirit and testing that claim with intelligence and determination will uncover an unexpected truth. Granted, the truth *is* a ghost in one case while, in the other, it's something embarrassingly ordinary. Still, when put side-by-side, these two legends reveal the kind of person best suited to go ghost hunting.

Athenodorus and the Telltale Bones

In part, Athenodorus is best understood as a *legendary* figure because of the difficulty in determining the *actual* person behind that legend. Think of Robin Hood. Various real-life persons have been hypothesized as being the legendary outlaw's model: Robert Hod, John Deyville, Roger Godberd, and others. At least, with Athenodorus, the name helps narrow things down, a point explained by D. Felton in her book *Haunted Greece and Rome: Ghost Stories from Classical Antiquity*. The first candidate is Athenodorus

Cordylion, and the second is Athenodorus Cananites. They both lived in the first century BCE; both were born in Tarsus and moved to Rome; both were philosophers belonging to the Stoic school. One might wonder if they ever crossed paths and chuckled over how much they had in common. In reference to Pliny's account, Felton says that "it is not possible to tell which Athenodorus was the protagonist here, or even if he was one of these two at all." Nonetheless, she confirms that the haunted house adventure probably took place "nearly one hundred years before Pliny was writing his letters."

Add to this long lapse of time the fact that Pliny almost certainly *heard* about Athenodorus's ghost hunt rather than *read* about it. The letter itself suggests that the tale was rooted in oral tradition. Felton points out that Pliny introduces the narrative by saying "I will tell it as I heard it," and subsequent sound effects and phrases affirm the idea that this story was circulated aloud.[1] Imagine a group of Romans at a fireside, sipping wine while swapping chilling tales. This particular one had been passed down for a very long time, yet there was still a ring of truth to it because the main character's name belonged to someone who had actually existed—and it's set in Athens, which is obviously real, too.

At the same time, with oral tradition, each narrator twists a plot point here or substitutes a detail there. The tale evolves over time, if only slightly. With this in mind, here is my own narration of Athenodorus's ghost hunt, tweaked and woven together from key translations of Pliny's transcription:[2]

There was at Athens a large and roomy house, which had a bad reputation and a sickly atmosphere. In the dead of night, a noise like iron clattering was often heard. Distant at first, it grew louder and more distinct as it moved nearer, eventually near enough to be identified as the rattling of chains. Soon afterward, a specter appeared in the form of an old man, extremely emaciated and squalid, with a long beard and disheveled hair. His feet were in shackles and his hands in manacles, the chains of which shook as he plodded forward.

The miserable residents passed their nights under the most dreadful terrors imaginable. Unable to sleep, their health suffered, exacerbating their fears and even bringing on death in some cases! Though the specter did not appear in the daytime, the impression of it remained so strong in their minds that it still seemed to stand before their eyes, keeping them in unrelenting anxiety. At length, the house was deserted, deemed absolutely uninhabitable, and abandoned entirely to the ghost.

However, in hopes that some tenant might be found who was ignorant of this dreadful situation, a notice was posted: the house was available either to be let or sold.

Athenodorus, the philosopher, then arrived in Athens. He came upon the advertisement and enquired about the price. It was remarkably affordable— suspiciously cheap! In a short time, he had learned the whole story of the haunting. Yet this did not discourage him. No, knowing the house's dark history only made him more strongly inclined to rent the place, and he promptly arranged to move into it.

He had barely done so when, as evening fell, he told his servants to place a couch in the front part of the house and to bring in a light along with his stylus and tablets. Next, he dismissed the servants, and they retired to the back. He knew that *expecting* to hear the metal rattling or to see the decrepit phantom could make him vulnerable to *imagining* those manifestations. To resist this, he kept his mind occupied by concentrating on his writing.

The first part of the night passed in complete silence. At length, though, Athenodorus heard a dim clanking of iron and then a more certain rattling of chains. He neither lifted up his eyes nor laid down his stylus. Instead, he mustered his resolve to remain calm and collected. The noise grew louder and advanced nearer. And *nearer!* It seemed to be just beyond the door. *Nearer!* Inside the room now! At last, Athenodorus looked up. There, he saw the ghost—exactly as wretched and horrible as it had been described to him.

And then, as the emaciated figure stood there, it did something unexpected. With a finger, it beckoned to the philosopher, as if bidding him to come closer.

Athenodorus had not heard about the ghost gesturing in this way. Well, he could do something unexpected, too! He replied to the ghost's invitation by raising his hand and signaling that it should wait a moment—he was busy—and then Athenodorus turned back to his writing tablet.

The ghost drew closer still. As if impatient, it moved close enough to rattle its chains over the head of this scribe so absorbed in his work. At this point, Athenodorus looked up and saw the ghost again beckon him to come closer or, as he now understood, to *follow.* Immediately, he rose and picked up a light, showing his willingness to follow the phantom.

The ghost slowly trudged out of the room, apparently weighted down with its chains. It walked as far as the property's courtyard, but no farther, for that's where it suddenly vanished. Finding himself alone, Athenodorus wisely marked the spot where the spirit had disappeared, using grass and leaves plucked from the grounds.

The next day, he informed the local magistrates about all that had happened and advised them to have some workers dig at the spot he had marked. As requested, an exhumation was performed.

The skeleton of a man in chains was found below that spot in the courtyard. The body must have lain buried there for a very long time because the bones were bare and the fetters corroded. The remains were gathered together and then buried at public expense with proper ceremony.

The house, thereafter, stood haunted no more.

Pliny included the Athenodorus narrative in a letter asking his reader, Lucius Licinius Sura (40-108 CE), what he thought about the possibility of such supernatural occurrences. It's sandwiched between another folkloric account of a grand prophetic vision and a strange tale that happened much closer to home. The latter involves two of Pliny's slaves dreaming about their hair being cut—and waking to find their hair *really had been cut!* He interprets this to be a personal prophecy about his escaping a difficult situation that, according to custom, would have required him to let his hair grow. Pliny admits to leaning toward believing all three stories, but his asking Sura's views reveals that the reality of such things was questioned even two thousand years ago.

Beyond being a test cast for the reality of the supernatural, though, the Athenodorus legend illustrates that ghosts—or fears more generally—might be easily eradicated when investigated with both emotion and imagination held in check. This is one of the principles of Stoic philosophy: strong emotions were founded on false judgments.[3] Athenodorus seems to know instinctively that the specter wasn't nearly as fearsome as the house's previous occupants had deemed it, a point especially emphasized when he calmly gestures for the ghost to wait. Furthermore, with a bit of figurative and literal digging, the ghost is revealed to be, not a monster, but the casualty of something monstrous. The tale works well as an instructive parable, then, instead of as a trustworthy report, as Pliny seemed to have seen it.

The Legacy of the Legend

Perhaps this flexibility in deciding exactly what to make of the Athenodorus legend played some part in it resonating with many readers in the 1800s, when it went through a bit of a revival, riding a wave of interest in ghosts. For scholars, English translations of Pliny's letters became widely available, and for students of Latin, textbooks offered the one addressed to Sura for practice. Translations of the legend also popped up in mainstream magazines. It was paraphrased in articles about ghosts published in America and in Britain, as well as in books on supernatural subjects. An elaborate retelling of the story was done as historical fiction, and by the time the 1900s arrived, a version even appeared in a storybook for children.[4] In other words, Athenodorus's ancient ghost hunt was introduced to a broad range of new readers.

One might wonder how much influence this revival of the old legend—especially its conclusion involving the telltale skeleton—had on haunted-house reports of the same period. There certainly are several hauntings connected to secret bones. A mansion called Hinton Ampner in Hampshire, England, was plagued by inexplicable sounds and spectral sights in the 1770s. The structure was demolished two decades later. Workers allegedly discovered a skull that seemed to belong to a monkey, but no expert ruling was made. By the 1940s, controversial ghost hunter Harry Price recounted the case and the workers' discovery, declaring, "Some say it was the skull of a baby!" Jump back to the 1870s. A clergyman living in a haunted house identified as "B— Lodge" claimed that the kitchen chimney had once caught fire and "what looked much like charred fragments of a child's bones came down." Now to 1897. Inexplicable noises and an apparition of an old man were experienced at a cottage outside the village of Halton Holgate in Lincolnshire, England. Newspapers reported that the manifestations were at least partly explained by the discovery of bones deemed "undoubtedly human" and "nearly 100 years old." Jump across the Atlantic. In 1871, investigators seeking a solution to a haunted tenement house in Kinderhook, New York, found "the bones of a human being" under one of the room's floorboards. In 1913, the new owner of a former roadhouse in Iowa found "fragments of human bones" while remodeling. The discovery reminded locals that, prior to the American Civil War, tales were told of the place being haunted.[5] Finding skeletal remains where they shouldn't be is certainly one of the few ways to substantiate a supernatural visitation with *hard* evidence.

And similar evidence was unearthed in at least two more cases, both of them involving celebrities. In 1848, the Fox sisters of Hydesville, New York, claimed they had communicated with the spirit of a murdered peddler, an assertion making headlines and igniting widespread interest in Spiritualism. About fifty years afterward, a skeleton was reported uncovered at their house, thrusting the Fox Sisters back into the news. One of the many reports says that "arm and leg bones of a human being" had been found first, followed by "all the other important bones of the body except the skull." This hints at a nearly complete skeleton, at least from the neck down. The reporter then adds, "This corroborates the statement of Margaret Fox, who had said that the spirit of a murdered man told her that his head had been severed from his body." However, a local physician named M.A. Veeder investigated and reported that, in actuality, the bones were a haphazard collection of "the forearm of *three* arms, in part—and some other odds and ends." In 1905, the doctor attributed the bones to a prankster with little knowledge of anatomy.[6]

Veeder's refutation appears to have slipped by Arthur

Conan Doyle, the author of the Sherlock Holmes mysteries. Once he had abandoned his popular detective and devoted himself to advocating Spiritualism, he recounted the Fox Sisters' saga along with the uncovering of the bones in his 1926 book *The History of Spiritualism.* According to Conan Doyle, those bones were decisive evidence, for they "proved beyond all doubt that someone had really been buried in the cellar of the Fox house." Curiously, he had bolstered one of his own ghost hunts in a similar manner in his 1918 work, *The New Revelation.* Here, he recalls having been part of an investigation team examining a poltergeist case at some point in the 1890s, but the team never cracked the case. "Some years afterward, however," he writes, "I met a member of the family who occupied the house, and he told me that after our visit the bones of a child, evidently long buried, had been dug up in the garden."[7] Was this genuine? Did either the family member or the mystery writer fabricate things to give the unsolved mystery a more satisfying conclusion, a finale following the pattern of the Athenodorus legend? Can the same be said for any of the other cases mentioned above?

Whatever the answers, there's one aspect of Athenodorus's investigation that helped establish and reinforce an element of ghost hunting that remains to this day: nocturnal surveillance. Holding a late-night stakeout is such a routine part of ghost hunting that it almost happens without a second thought. During such an investigation, we might say a ghost hunter must remain *vigilant.* The word is traced back to the Latin *vigil,* meaning awake, alert, and watching. It might have been used to describe a sentinel dutifully standing watch. Meanwhile, the Latin *virilia* translates to what we now call *vigil,* such as when a group holds a candlelight vigil. Such ceremonies serve various purposes, but one is to remember the dead. Vigils commonly occur in the evening or, perhaps, when participants would otherwise be sleeping. Athenodorus, in other words, was vigilantly holding a vigil as he kept watch for a ghost by night.

In this regard, one might argue that Pliny offers us the oldest known ghost-hunter story. The Athenodorus legend is not the first ghost story, though—not even the first one of which we have a written record. Pliny's transcription is one of three extant haunted-house stories from Classical antiquity, according to Felton, who adds, "There may have been many variations that simply do not survive." Of those three, a tale told in Plautus's comedy *Mostellaria* is the earliest.[8] Nonetheless, it's remarkable how the basic methods of ghost hunting have remained much the same. Thousands have followed Athenodorus by waiting until nightfall, entering a spot alleged to be haunted, sacrificing sleep—and, some would say, common sense—all in pursuit of something ghostly. Given its legacy, Athenodorus's act of nocturnal surveillance is, to be sure, legendary.

Deshoulières Yanks Off the Sheet

In France during the late 1600s, Deshoulières was well known as a poet. Her writing brought her accolades, the patronage of King Louis XIV, and friendships with her country's literary elite. If this seems unusual for a woman in that century—it was, of course—but her intelligence and talent were allowed to flourish in part by her being associated with the libertine subculture. In Deshoulières's case, according to Christopher H. Johnson, libertinism was less about sexual freedom and more about freedom from traditional gender constraints. He says that "women seeking intellectual fulfillment" were able to mingle in "a world of salons, theater, discussion groups, and poetry-reading circles where men and women could act more or less on equal footing."[9] In this setting, Deshoulières participated in the era's debates about literature, social politics, and philosophy.

Her philosophical views were expressed in her poetry, and it is there that we see her as a voice for materialism. As

John J. Conley explains, Deshoulières wrote poems

> to argue that natural causes can adequately explain such apparently spiritual phenomena as thought, volition, and love. In metaphysics, Deshoulières argues that the real is comprised of variations of matter and that material causation adequately explains observed changes in the real. In anthropology, she claims that the difference between animal and human is one of degree, not of kind. Material organs, and not the occult powers of a spiritual soul, produce such human phenomena as thought and choice.[10]

Perhaps an easy way to grasp this philosophy to think of it as science-minded skepticism aimed at explanations that lean on the supernatural or spiritual.

Here's an example. In one of the Sherlock Holmes stories, the great detective accepts a case that *seems* to involve a vampire. Very much *unlike* Conan Doyle in his later years, Holmes promptly pooh-poohs the idea: "This agency stands flat-footed upon the ground, and there it must remain. The world is big enough for us. No ghosts need apply."[11] I'm not giving anything away by saying that Holmes' disbelief helps him uncover the truth behind the mystery, and while such a perspective might strike one as too narrow for a ghost hunter, we'll see that many of the pre-Victorian ghost hunters in this book exhibited a healthy strain of skepticism.

In fact, much as the Athenodorus legend provides a role model for Stoic philosophy, the story of Deshoulières's ghost hunt acts as a dramatization of how materialism—looking for physical explanations to phenomena alleged to be supernatural—can lead to the truth. Despite their different destinations, the two tales follow the same basic path: 1) unusual events in a human habitation lead to a reputation of it being fearfully haunted; 2) a brave, calm investigator performs nocturnal surveillance in that spot; 3) that investigator discovers something other than what people had thought; and 4) the mystery is solved. In a sense, Deshoulières is a direct descendent of Athenodorus, even though her case ends on an entirely *natural* note.

The poet's parable circulated in the early 1800s in a variety of publications.[12] Was there a historical basis to it? Are there are any earlier records of it? Was it shared via oral tradition? I'll step aside and eagerly await those answers to come from other researchers. For now, here is another of my own patchworks of what, at least for now, I'll call the *legend* of Deshoulières's ghost hunt:

Madame Deshoulières accepted an invitation to the château of Count and Countess de Larnville, which was several miles from Paris. There, she was offered her choice of any bedrooms in the château—except for one. The forbidden room, she learned, was visited by strange sounds at night. Worse yet, some who had slept there reported being touched by the "fleshly arm" of an otherwise disembodied phantom!

On hearing about the terrible things that had happened in this room, Deshoulières immediately insisted upon sleeping there.

The Count and Countess were aghast! The host did his best to dissuade his guest from asking such a thing, and when this failed, the hostess redoubled the effort. (In some versions, Countess de Larnville points out that Deshoulières is pregnant and would be putting her fetus at risk.) However, no amount of warning could stop Deshoulières from restating her desire to confront the supposed horror of that eerie bedroom. Horrified yet gracious, the de Larnvilles acquiesced to their visitor's wishes.

The room was grand, its fireplace was huge, and the windows were shadowed by the château's deep walls.

Deshoulières bid the chambermaid to light a large candle and dismissed her, something like Athenodorus sending his servants away. Rather than focus on some writing, though, the poet started reading a book. Perhaps following the example of those who claimed to have encountered the ghost, she allowed herself to drift off to sleep.

But Deshoulières became instantly alert when she heard the door open. Quiet footsteps followed—footsteps creeping into the room. *The candle must have burned itself out,* she realized. *And yet I remember the maid locking the door.*

Deshoulières challenged the intruder, saying that she wasn't afraid and had every intention of exposing whoever was pretending to be a ghost. Apparently, however, the hoaxer was just as fearless. She did not receive a reply.

She also did not flinch when the intruder then knocked against a screen close to the bed. Next, the prowler somehow caused the draperies to slide along the rod, making a sharp sound that could have been interpreted as a ghostly scream to someone more terrified. The ghost hunter only grew more intrigued.

On the hunch that she might be dealing with one of the servants, Deshoulières again declared that she wasn't scared and would reveal the culprit to the de Larnvilles.

Again, her words were met with silence.

Well, not *silence* exactly. The faux-phantom was being pretty noisy. It clumsily knocked against a heavy stand used for candles, and that fell with a loud clang. Next, it must have plopped against the foot of the bed because, even through the mattress, Deshoulières felt the frame bumped.

She still wasn't sure what it was, but this was her opportunity! She swung around to the far side of the

15

bed and reached for the intruder. She grabbed what felt like two velvety ears and held them firmly. Whoever— or, more likely, *whatever*—those ears belonged to didn't mind this at all.

By now, Deshoulières was fairly certain she had solved the mystery of the spooky noises and alarming touches others had experienced in that room. Absolute proof was needed, however, so she kept a hand on her furry prisoner despite the fact that doing so kept her awake and painfully positioned for hours.

Finally, sunrise came, and even those deep, shadowed windows allowed in enough light for the poet to confirm her suspicion.

It was the dog.

Named Gros-Blanc (or Big-White), the large pet was a loyal and friendly favorite at the château. Rather than being annoyed with having had its ears held all night, Gros-Blanc licked Deshoulières's hands, apparently in appreciation for her having kept them warm.

Meanwhile, the de Larnvilles had spent a sleepless night, worrying about their guest. They even imagined that the poet might be found dead in the morning, and to relieve their anxiety, as soon as propriety allowed, they went straight to the room. They didn't know whether to cringe or laugh when they learned what had caused all the mischief.

"I honestly thought it was the ghost of my mother," confessed the Count. "She died shortly before the, uh, *supernatural* visitor appeared."

"If I hadn't held him to the floor all night," said Deshoulières with a chuckle, "this supernatural visitor would have been my bedfellow. But there's one more mystery—easily accounted for, I suspect."

Deshoulières then examined the door's lock. The wood around it had rotted enough that a moderate push would have rendered it useless. And Gros-Blanc was big enough to have given the door a moderate push. The reports of a restless ghost were put to rest.

Most of the versions I've discovered end with a rather heavy-handed explanation of what readers ought to have learned from the anecdote. Be like Deshoulières: courageous, persistent, and smart. Be neither gullible nor superstitious. This moral-to-the-story, along with the story's basic parallels to the Athenodorus narrative, reinforce the idea that this is more a work of illustrative folklore and less some biographical tidbit.

The Ghost of a Debunker

Perhaps more subtly, the Deshoulières legend also teaches a lesson in materialism. While Athenodorus pulled the sheet off a terrifying ghost to find a sympathetic one underneath, Deshoulières exposed a terrifying ghost to be a corporeal pooch. In other words, the poet used a basic ghost-hunting technique to debunk reports of a ghost, reinforcing a materialist viewpoint. Clearly, that was in keeping with *some* people's philosophical thinking in the late 1600s. Others, of course, would have favored a more traditionally religious message, one reinforcing the principle that inter-action between the physical and supernatural realms occurs in God hearing and acting upon prayers, in divine justice ensuring that evil deeds be punished, in Satan influencing worldly events, and even in ghosts appearing.

But why was this parable of materialism published in multiple sources in the early 1800s? Conley explains, "In the decades following her death, Deshoulières was acclaimed as a bold philosophical thinker who prepared the path to the religious skepticism of the Enlightenment."[13] On the one hand, the Age of Enlightenment was marked by a rise in scientific progress, in trusting one's own senses, and in rejecting dogmatic thinking—and on the other, it initiated a push toward greater liberty, toward constitutional government, and toward a separation of church and state. Putting dates on this revolutionary period of history is difficult, but 1700 to 1800 provides a rough idea. More germane to this book, ghosts went underground toward the end of the Enlightenment era.

Indeed, open your 1797 edition of the *Encyclopedia Britannica* and flip to "Specter." After discussing ghosts in the Bible, in ancient Rome and Greece, and in cultures across the world—after an examination of logical problems with ghosts as presented in allegedly true reports (e.g., why do they so often appear only at night?)—the writer expounds upon a list of natural causes that account for sightings. They are: 1) misperceptions caused by the dark and by fear; 2) dreams mistaken for reality, an error made especially by superstitious people; 3) opium; 4) hypochondria, hysteria, or madness; 5) drunkenness; and 6) hoaxes. A couple of years later, an article appeared in *The Monthly Magazine* that offers a more physiological explanation for ghosts. Identified only as P.W., the writer opens by asking how reports of ghosts from reliable witnesses can be reconciled with "sound reason and the established laws of nature." The proposed answer is that such sightings result from a glitch between the optic nerve and the brain. "We experience the same thing," says P.W., "on receiving a violent blow to the face, when we imagine we see a great number of sparks before our eyes. Thus, different pressures and motions may also produce different notions, which have no external efficient object." In other words, anyone can see what *isn't* there at times. The writer supports this idea with several examples of vision gone wrong. The closest one that comes to something like a ghost involves an elderly man claiming to have seen a girl when others in the room saw nothing. In the next few decades, though, respected physicians focused more on ghost sightings and further developed the thesis that these are attributable to physiological conditions.[14] Of course, those doctors' books presumably had a far narrower readership than the encyclopedia and magazine mentioned above.

It is interesting to note that, in the 1790s, even popular fiction was employing physical causes to explain and debunk any and all ghost sightings. Doing so was the hallmark of Ann Radcliffe, whose Gothic romances made her, in the words of some, the most popular writer of her time. Radcliffe routinely tantalized readers with seemingly supernatural events but then gave them earthbound explanations. In 1826, a critic looking back at Radcliffe's novels first wonders why someone as talented as her "should, in all her works intended for publication, studiously resolve the circumstances, by which she has excited superstitious apprehensions, into mere physical causes." He explains why this technique *shouldn't* work in fiction, but then says that it "sets off, in the strongest light, the wizard power of her genius"—after all, readers loved what she was writing. Indeed, early in the next century, in a book titled *Apparitions; or, The Mystery of Ghosts, Hobgoblins, and Haunted Houses, Developed* Joseph Taylor anthologized stories that follow the same outline: scary situations are shown to be the product of superstition, gullibility, or the imagination gone awry.[15] Some of the tales are introduced as true, but presumably many of them are not—or, at least, they are well-traveled folktales. The Deshoulières legend would have fit perfectly.

Obviously, there was an audience for such tales in the early 1800s, even if the real-life model for the protagonist had been dead for more than a century. The same had happened with Athenodorus. In fact, that span of time might have made these legends all the more compelling. A listener or reader could ask, "Who's around to say they *didn't* really happen?"

¹ Felton, D., *Haunted Greece and Rome: Ghost Stories from Classical Antiquity,* U. of Texas Press, 1999, pp. 67-68, 65.

² The long history of translations includes William Melmoth's in *The Letters of Pliny the Consul with Occasional Remarks,* vol. 2 (Printed for R. Dodsley, 1747) pp. 421-424; John Delaware Lewis's in *The Letters of the Younger Pliny* (Kegan Paul, Trench,Trübner & Co., 1890) pp. 245-246; and Felton's, p. 65-66.

³ Dirk Baltzly states, "The Stoics did, in fact, hold that emotions like fear or envy . . . either were, or arose from, false judgements and that the sage—a person who had attained moral and intellectual perfection—would not undergo them." "Stoicism," *The Stanford Encyclopedia of Philosophy* (Spring 2019 Edition), edited by Edward N. Salta, https://plato.stanford.edu/archives/spr2019/entries/stoicism.

⁴ See footnote 3 above for scholarly translations. Textbooks for students of Latin include Alfred J. Church's *Latin Prose Lessons* (Bell and Daldy, 1862) p. 60, and J.H. Allen and J.B. Greenough's *A Method of Instruction in Latin* (Ginn Brother, 1875) pp. 63-64. The translations in popular magazines include M.L.B.'s "A Haunted House at Athens," *Mirror of Literature, Amusement, and Instruction* 15 (May 22, 1830) pp. 339-340, and "Haunted House at Athens," *Iris* 1 (June 1841) pp. 393-394. The American magazine article surveying ghosts is "Prophetic Spectres," *Bizarre* 4 (December 3, 1853) pp. 137-138, and the British one is Edwin Sharpe Grew's "Famous Ghosts," *Ludgate* 4 (July 1897) pp. 257-258. The books on supernatural topics are Augustine Calmet's *The Phantom World,* vol. 1 (Richard Bentley, 1850) pp. 242-243, and John Netten Radcliffe's *Fiends, Ghosts, and Sprites* (Richard Bentley, 1854) pp. 74-75. The historical-fiction retelling is H.W. Herbert's "Athenodorus in the Haunted House," *Godey's Magazine and Lady's Book* 34.1 (January 1847) pp. 33-36. The children's version is Mrs. [Leonora Blanche] Lang's "An Old-world Ghost," *The Strange Story Book* (Longmans, Green, and Co., 1913) pp. 79-84.

⁵ The primate skull at Hinton Ampner is discussed in "A Hampshire Ghost Story," *Gentlemen's Magazine* 9 (December 1872) p. 667, and Harry Price's exclamation that it was said to be a child's is in *Poltergeist over England: Three Centuries of Mischievous Ghosts* (Country Life Ltd., 1945) p. 144. The charred bones are mentioned—and negated by another witness—in Frank Podmore's "An Account of Some Abnormal Phenomena Alleged to Have Occurred at B— Lodge, W—," *Journal of the Society for Psychical Research* 2 (February 1886) p. 198, 206. The newspaper reports about the Halton Holgate case are reproduced in James John Hissey's *Over Fen and Wold* (Macmillan, 1898) pp. 278-

279. The two American cases are covered in "Skeleton Found in a Haunted House," *Democratic Press* [Ravenna, Ohio], January 26, 1871, p. 1, and "Finding Bones Revives Tales," *Decorah Public Opinion* [Iowa], June 11, 1913, p. 5.

[6] The newspaper article appears in "Cannot Find Skull," *New York Tribune*, November 24, 1904, p. 10. Dr. Veeder's findings were published in "Correspondence," *Occult Review* 2 (July 1905) p. 52, and elaborated on in "Editorial," *Journal of the American Society for Psychical Research* 3 (March 1909) p. 191.

[7] Conan Doyle's two accounts of telltale bones are in *A History of Spiritualism*, vol. 1 (George H. Doran, 1926) p. 73 and *The New Revelation* (George H. Doran, 1918) p. 35.

[8] Felton, pp. 40, 50.

[9] Christopher H. Johnson, *Becoming Bourgeois: Love, Kinship, and Power in Provincial France, 1670–1880* (Cornell UP, 2015) p. 54.

[10] John J. Conley, "Deshoulières, Antoinette du Ligier de la Garde (1638-1694)," *Internet Encyclopedia of Philosophy: A Peer-Reviewed Academic Resource,* https://iep.utm.edu/deshouli/.

[11] Arthur Conan Doyle, "The Adventure of the Sussex Vampire," *Strand* 67 (January 1924) p. 4.

[12] British sources include "Madame Deshoulieres, the French Poetess," *Literary Gazette*, no. 46 (December 6, 1817) pp. 363-364; "The Ghost Discovered," *Repository of Arts, Literature, Fashions, Manufactures, &c.* 5 (January 1, 1818) pp. 38-40; and Shoto and Reuben Percy [Joseph Clinton Robertson and Thomas Byerley], "Seizing a Ghost," *Percy Anecdotes* (Printed for T. Boys, 1820) pp. 136-140. Afterward, the anecdote re-materialized in the U.S. via Sarah Josepha Hale's entry for Deshoulières in *Woman's Record; or, Sketches of All Distinguished Women* (Harper & Brothers, 1853) p. 288, and May Mannering's "A Ghost Story," *Our Boys and Girls* 2 (August 10, 1867) pp. 399-401.

[13] Conley.

[14] "Spectre," *Encyclopedia Britannica*, vol. 17 (printed for A. Bell and C. Macfarquar, 1797) pp. 677-684. P.W., "On Apparitions and Second Sight," *Monthly Magazine* 8 (November 1799) pp. 780-783. Books proposing physiological causes for ghost sightings include John Ferriar's *An Essay towards a Theory of Apparitions* (Printed for Cadel and Davies by J. and J. Haddock, 1813) and John Alderson's *An Essay on Apparitions, in which Their Appearance Is Accounted for by Causes Wholly Independent of Preternatural Agency* (Printed for Longman, et al., 1823).

---

¹⁵ Thomas Noon Talfourd, "Memoir of the Life and Writings of Mrs. Radcliffe," in *Gastone de Blondeville; or, The Court of Henry III Keeping Festival in Arden,* by Ann Radcliffe, vol. 1 (Henry Colburn, 1826) pp. 115-117. Joseph Taylor, *Apparitions; or, The Mystery of Ghosts, Hobgoblins, and Haunted Houses, Developed* (Printed for Lackington, Allen, and Co., 1814).

CHAPTER TWO

PARSONS IN THE FIELD

Cornwall sits at the southwestern tip of Britain. It is rich in ghostlore, and a curious thread involves the *laying* of ghosts. Laying a ghost means finding a way to let it rest or, in particularly disagreeable hauntings, to banish the spirit with exorcism. There are several stories that suggest the most proficient ghost-layers are Anglican parsons.

One shining example is the Reverend Mr. Polkinghorne. It was said that, when others failed, Parson Polkinghorne could be counted upon to make nasty phantoms disappear for good. He did exactly that after being asked to assist with a haunted mansion in a village called Treen. The ruinous building was invaded by disembodied screams, eerie laughter, and a stench seeming to come from the grave. No one but Parson Polkinghorne and the clergyman who had sought his guidance ever saw *how* the two evicted the otherworldly intruders, but it involved some large books and a length of rope.[1] Maybe, after an incantation or two, the pair of preachers were able to lasso the ghosts.

My source for the Polkinghorne legend, published in 1873, gives a hazy "[t]hree or four centuries ago" as a timeframe for the adventure. Another ghost-busting parson of legend can be more solidly fixed. The Reverend Thomas Flavell died on October 26, 1682, having served at Mullion Village. Instead of a rope to wrangle wraiths, Flavell was said to combine books on divination and on the black arts with other tools. When a servant pried into one of those

23

books, she released a hoard of evil spirits, which then attacked her. Intuitively, the preacher interrupted his sermon to go rescue her. Reciting passages from the esoteric volume backwards while brandishing his walking stick, he conquered the demons. In another story, Flavell was seen cracking a whip to corral unwelcome specters.[2] At times, these legendary men who drove away supernatural varmints seem worthy of the name the Clerical Cowboys of Cornwall.

There *is* a posse of them, too, with names such as Jago, Corker, Woods, and Richards. Following in Athenodorus's footsteps, these figures endured and evolved in oral tradition. They were then put on paper long after the period when the original events supposedly took place. However, the supernatural entities these parsons faced often feel more like demons than spirits traceable to someone who had once lived in the area. The legends of Parson Dodge and Parson Ruddle, on the other hand, clearly involve ghosts of former residents. Put side by side, this pair's exploits illustrate a vital decision any good paranormal investigator must make: is the haunting entity lingering in the physical realm because it's here to do *harm,* or is it here seeking *help?*

Parson Dodge and the Heedless Phantom

Spirits out to do harm knew all too well about the powerful exorcist Parson Dodge, and they dreaded running into him. At least, that's how the clergyman was remembered decades after his death. In an 1823 history of the Cornish boroughs of East and West Looe, Thomas Bond devotes a couple of paragraphs to Dodge, who ministered at Talland, a village on the southern coast. Bond says that the parson was, "by traditional accounts, a very singular man. He had the reputation of being deeply skilled in the black art, and could raise ghosts, or send them into the Red Sea, at the nod of his head." Many of these spirits "were seen, in all sorts of shapes, flying and running before [Dodge], and he pursuing them, with his whip, in a most daring manner." Bond ends the short profile by presenting the inscription on a tombstone one could visit in the Talland churchyard:

> Here lieth the body of the Rev. Mr. Richard Dodge, late of Talland, Vicar, who departed this life the 13th day of January 1746, in the 93rd year of his age.[3]

Dodge, it seems, was real. Eighty years after his death, though, he had evolved into an ecclesiastical superhero, the stuff of legend.

In fact, one of Dodge's encounters with a particularly fearsome ghost was published in 1865. Thomas Q. Couch says he heard it "by a country fire-side," certainly a great way to hear any folktale. He then set it to paper and titled it "The Spectral Coach."[4] Couch's transcription provides far more exposition and detail than is typical for a fireside ghost story, so I felt free to condense it here:

> In the early 1700s, a messenger arrived at Talland Church and asked to see the Reverend Mr. Dodge. The parson was a remarkable man with heavy eyebrows crowning serious eyes. He wore a dignified periwig and somber black apparel. Dodge was known as a staunch opponent to the area's many smugglers, who took advantage of Talland's seaside locale and who saw their crimes as little more than a viable trade. Still, while the smugglers rarely heeded Dodge's lecturing, they listened to him with respect, knowing that this was a kind and honest man.
>
> The smugglers were probably more awestruck by the parson's skills at ridding Talland of supernatural visitors. Some of these were ghosts troubled by sins committed in life. Others were evil spirits intent on tempting the villagers into committing such sins or simply around to make life hellish.

It was this remarkable man who greeted the messenger by asking, "Well, my good man, what brings you hither?"

"A letter, please your reverence, from Mr. Grylls of Lanreath."

Dodge knew Grylls as a fellow clergyman and a good friend. He read and re-read the letter carefully. It concerned a stretch of moorland. A few years earlier, two squires had fought over this property in an effort to secure legal ownership of it. The land wasn't especially valuable, but their much poorer neighbors regularly used it as a common area for grazing and the like. The attraction of ownership was the prospect of *denying* these lowly laborers that privilege, and for that dubious honor, the two squires battled viciously.

One of the squires was old enough that he should have been more worried about what property he would leave behind than about what he could acquire. Nonetheless, after eagerly awaiting the results of his latest lawsuit for the contested land, he learned that he had *lost* the case. His devastation was so deep that it might have hastened his death.

Yet even death did not stop his craving to control that land!

Grylls explained that a number of the locals— people he knew to be honest and reliable—had reported seeing the ghost of the land-hungry squire driving a black coach across that moor. The witnesses described the apparition as dressed in black, too, and leading a team of *headless* horses!

The letter ended with a plea for Dodge's help. Could he come verify or debunk the haunting? If it was real, might he do what he was so famous for by convincing or compelling the spirit to stop clinging to this world? Grylls closed by saying his messenger could supply any needed details.

After studying the letter, Dodge looked up. He did indeed want more information. The messenger, who was the Lanreath church's sexton, hadn't personally seen the spectral coach. Neither had Grylls, for that matter, but the sexton had heard the sounds of a coach one night. He could only explain it as being the same unearthly black coach that so many of his neighbors would swear to have encountered. The haunted moor was called Blackadon, and it was about two miles outside the village.

Dodge nodded, bid his handmaid to feed the sexton, and sat down to write a response. Obligations prevented him from joining the investigation right away, he wrote, but he would be there in two days' time.

Those two days passed. Parsons Dodge and Grylls rode to Blackadon and reached it around 10 o'clock at night. By day, the distant farmhouses helped relieve the desolation of the place, if only a bit. At night, those homes were lost in darkness, and the land felt utterly bleak and barren. The wind moaned through the few trees. Mingling with it was faint howling, hopefully nothing more than dogs at those farms far away.

Both clergymen called upon their faith to muster the courage needed to proceed. With barely a word, they led their horses forward. They wandered this way, that way, and they split then reunited, split then reunited. In a way, it was a night perfectly suited for confronting a spectral coach, but neither parson did so. No greedy ghost was seen or heard. Not a single decapitated horse trotted past them.

At last, the two men decided to resume their ghost hunt another night. Saying goodnight, Grylls headed to his rectory in Lanreath while Dodge took a shortcut, intending to make his way back to Talland.

Something strange happened a short time later.

Dodge had reached the bottom of a valley—when his mare stopped. She reared backwards, and she staggered sideways, and she stood solid. The parson did all he could to coax the horse to move forward, yet with no success. It occurred to him that this might be a sign from Heaven that he should go back. The horse complied with that. In fact, the mare carried Dodge back to Blackadon at a speed that was downright dangerous!

Again, the horse reached a point where she came to an unyielding standstill. It was at this very instant when Dodge glimpsed *an unmoving, black coach* ahead of him. His mare was seized with fury, and the parson struggled to keep from being thrown while also squinting to make out a terrible sight. Not only was the team at rest in front of the black coach *headless*—not only was the driver *dressed in black*—but his friend Grylls was lying on the ground before them, apparently *unconscious or worse!*

Parson Dodge breathed deeply, quelling his panic and struggling to remember the appropriate prayer. Reciting the holy words seemed to fortify his own courage as well as his horse's. Together, they strode fearlessly toward the spectral coach.

When Dodge was close enough, it was the ghost's turn to panic. Suddenly, it shouted, "Dodge is come! I must be gone!" The phantom lashed the reigns. The monstrous horses charged forward. Within seconds, the apparition disappeared into the darkness.

Not too long afterward, a group of Lanreath villagers arrived to find Dodge comforting his friend in his arms. They explained that they had awoken to a riderless horse covered with sweat and galloping through the streets. They easily recognized it as Grylls's and quickly concluded that something awful had spooked the horse and left Grylls behind. This was all they needed to band together and search for their parson, even if it meant going to Blackadon, where Grylls had said he and Dodge were headed.

But Grylls was in shock, unable to tell what he had seen. It took several days for him to recover. At some point, Parson Dodge returned to his duties in Talland.

Exactly where the spectral coach, its fanatical driver, and the team of ghastly horses went, no one really knew. All the Lanreath residents could say—and they did so with great relief—was that the squire had finally relinquished his claim on that stretch of barren moorland.

Is there a moral to this story? Don't become too attached to earthly possessions because, even if you stand your ground after death, you can't take them with you. Or maybe the point is that God's representatives will ensure you can't have what you don't deserve. One's reputation can be just as powerful as one's actions? Something like that.

It almost doesn't matter because, instead of a parable, this seems more designed to be simply a gripping ghost story, especially suited to tantalize an audience gathered around a fire. The squire's covetous character is established up front while he's still alive, only to become far more horrifying once he's a ghost. He works as a one-dimensional villain, in other words, without any explanation of how he became so villainous. The setting is also chosen to evoke fear. Instead of a haunted house or room—one which might be cozy *if not for* the ghost—this legend is mostly set in a desolate region that would be eerie *even without* the ghost. For good measure, the tale also draws from a spooky tradition of spectral coaches and headless horses that guarantees chilling entertainment even in a story that doesn't have much at all to do with coaches, horses, or headlessness.

A Herd of Headless Horses

Phantom coaches drawn by headless horses seem not to materialize very often in the 21st century. Perhaps these vehicular spirits have been replaced by hitchhiking ghosts. However, the legend Couch says he heard in the mid-1800s was probably shaped by various reports of similar coaches and horses. For instance, as folklorist John Gunn says in an 1849 book, "The marvellous account of a carriage drawn by headless horses at the seat of the Fastolfs, Caistor Castle, is not yet utterly discarded." The ruins of this castle can still be visited in Norfolk, England, which was also home to Blickling Hall, former residence of the Boleyn family. While Anne Boleyn is well-known for being beheaded by King Henry VIII, an 1854 book notes that the headless specter of Anne's *father*—or perhaps her *brother,* who was also decapitated—are said to annually appear in a coach pulled by horses similarly inconvenienced. That same year, Cuthbert Bede added several more examples, including a Devonshire clergyman who had retained his own head while the four horses who pulled his coach had not.[5]

The phenomena was present in the previous century, too. In 1787, Francis Grose blamed stories about the supernatural heard in childhood on the persistence of a variety of superstitions. Turning to beliefs about spirits of the departed in "former times," he explains: "Ghosts of superior rank, when they appeared abroad, rode in coaches drawn by six headless horses, and driven by a headless coachman and postilions." The earliest specific case—albeit, told third-hand—that I've located is from 1711. That's when Joseph Addison recalled a butler telling him about a footman who "had been almost frightened out of his Wits by a Spirit that appear'd to him in the Shape of a black Horse without an Head."[6] Therefore, the legend of Dodge's encounter on Blackadon incorporated a narrative element at least a century old.

Such equine enigmas did not stop at the English border, though. An 1826 issue of *The Glasgow Chronicle* reported that residents of Paisley, Scotland, had witnessed "carts, caravans, and coaches" drawn by headless horses and, in some cases, moving without any horses at all. A woman in Wales regularly commuted "from Tenby to Sampson Cross Roads, near Stackpole," driven by a coachman, accompanied by a footman, and pulled by four horses—all of them ghosts and all of them headless—according to an 1885 article. Phantom coaches and decapitated specters seem to have been especially common over in Ireland. In 1870, John O'Hanlon listed where such apparitions typically appeared. They might approach or depart a cemetery, usually around midnight. If spotted circling a house, then one of its residents would likely die. "These spectres," he continues, "are often found passing near the spot, where some murder has been committed, or where a fatal accident occurred." On the pressing question of what happens to the missing parts, O'Hanlon explains: "The heads of men and horses are sometimes seen completely detached from the corresponding bodies. Oftentimes these heads alone are observed flying through the air."[7] While Parson Dodge witnessing that coach on Blackadon was not as common as, say, seeing a hearse pass by, such sightings were well established across the United Kingdom in the 1800s.

And headless horsemen were said to ride on the other sides of the Channel and the Atlantic. One wound its way among the Hartz Mountains in northern Germany, for example, and another through the Cumberland Mountains in the eastern U.S. Though it's fiction rather than folklore, we mustn't forget the decapitated fellow who chased Ichabod Crane out of Sleepy Hollow (but, as careful readers of Washington Irving's tale will tell you, that was probably Brom Bones in a clever disguise).[8] Be they headless horses or headless *riders,* these creatures had quite an impressive range.

The point is, however, that the story of Parson Dodge's ghost hunt is something different from the legends of Athenodorus and Deshoulières. The Dodge narrative doesn't teach a lesson in relying on calm, cool-headed reason to see the truth behind a haunting previously deemed malevolent. Indeed, Blackadon moor *was* visited by a malevolent ghost, one intent upon terrorizing the locals and, in the case of Parson Grylls, doing harm. The presence of the headless horses towing that spectral coach heightens this evil intent.

If there's any lesson for ghost hunters here, perhaps it's about putting in the time and doing the homework needed to build as impressive a reputation as Parson Dodge. Only then can one efficiently eradicate such wickedness.

Parson Ruddle and the Spectral Messenger

In 1720, a pamphlet was printed that includes the narrative of Parson Ruddle successfully laying the ghost of Dorothy Dingly in the Cornish borough of Launceton. The pamphlet is very clear about *when* the main events of the haunting had happened: Ruddle conducted a funeral on June 20, 1665, which is when he first met the father of the family concerned in the haunting. He vanquished Dingly's spirit on July 29 of the same year. The pamphlet was published 55 years after the fact, and this appears to be the first time the story was available to a wide audience. The tale was retold in 1817—almost exactly the same but for the addition of some useful names and places—in C.S. Gilbert's *An Historical Survey of the County of Cornwall*. Now, it's about a century-and-a-half after the original events.

As discussed in the previous chapter, the early 1800s was a time of strong skepticism regarding the reality of ghosts. But this view was reevaluated as the century proceeded, and so were historical chronicles about ghostly encounters. A debate rose over whether the Ruddle narrative was a work of flat-out fiction or something much more truthful. For several decades, the chronicle was assumed to be a work of fiction written by Daniel Defoe, better known as the author of *Robinson Crusoe* (1719). In 1898, though, Alfred F. Robbins argued that Ruddle himself was the author, and to prove that it wasn't simply a product of Defoe's imagination, Robbins set forth several interesting claims regarding the authenticity of the central figures in the haunting. Records exist, he says, of a John Ruddle having ministered at Saint Mary Magdalene in Launceston, Cornwall, from 1663 to 1699. There is even a monument there to confirm it. He also worked as a master at the Launceton Free School, having earned a Master of Arts at Caius College, Cambridge. Other names in the 1720 and 1817 versions fit the time and place, too. Sabine Baring-Gould repeated these claims in 1909—adding a portrait that he claims depicts Ruddle![9]

Unfortunately, Robbins provides only scraps of hard-to-locate documentation to support his claims, and that portrait comes from Baring-Gould's personal collection instead of a gallery where others can examine it. The notion that some of the people mentioned in the chronicle were real is certainly reasonable, but even Robbins suggests that the core narrative might be a bit iffy when he admits, "'Facts' as concerning a ghost story would not seem to be customary."[10] Again, we're in legend territory.

Following and abridging the 1720 version—and borrowing the names found in the 1817 one—I present my rendition of the legend of Parson Ruddle's encounter with the ghost of Dorothy Dingly:

In early 1665, a disease spread through Launceton, and some of the students there died of it. One victim was sixteen-year-old John Eliott, a clever and handsome young man. On his deathbed, John had requested that his schoolmaster, Parson Ruddle, perform the funeral service, and that sad day came on

June 20. The clergyman's eulogy was designed both to endear the memory of the deceased to his survivors and to illustrate how John had been a model for the other students to follow.

After the service, the parson was approached by an elderly man, someone Ruddle hadn't met before. The old man introduced himself as Mr. Bligh and invited Ruddle to visit his farmhouse, named Botathen. Bligh asked if the parson could visit *that night,* but the parson was unable to come until the following Monday. Even so, the old man sent a message asking if Ruddle could come on *Sunday.* Clearly, Bligh or someone in his family was in need of spiritual guidance, but why was the actual problem being kept secret?

When Ruddle arrived at Botathen, he was introduced to Mrs. Bligh and, unexpectedly, to another clergyman named Williams. After much hesitation, this other parson and the Blighs explained the dilemma. The Blighs had a son named Sam, who was about the age of the late John Eliott. Over the last several months, Sam had grown melancholy and sullen. He told farfetched stories about being haunted by an evil spirit in the form of a woman, insisting the phantom waited in a field that he passed while walking to school. He ran away when she came in his direction, so he said. The parents' thinking was that their son was lazy and making up excuses to avoid his classes—or, perhaps, this was some ploy to escape rural Cornwall and go visit his brother in London. But if Sam honestly *did* believe he was seeing ghosts, how could they convince him it was all just a delusion? They wanted Parson Ruddle's advice on how to proceed.

"I need to know more details," said Ruddle. "Your son's talk of ghosts is certainly strange, but not necessarily beyond belief. Let me talk to the lad. If I can get him to trust me, I might be in a better position to tell you what I think."

Without a moment's delay, Mr. Bligh and his wife called for their son to come at once. Ruddle walked with the boy to a nearby orchard, putting distance between themselves and the others. Thinking he would have to win the boy's confidence first, Ruddle discovered that, no, Sam was completely open and honest. He *liked* attending classes and had *no* desire to miss them by leaving Cornwall. That wasn't what was troubling him. It was—exactly as he said—a weird phantom lurking in a field and seemingly waiting for him. Well, that and the fact that his parents refused to believe he had encountered a ghost.

Perhaps it was seeing that Ruddle kept an open mind about what he was saying that made Sam continue. "I recognize the ghost. She was a neighbor who died about eight years ago. Her size and shape, her age, even her complexion matches Dorothy Dingly. I can't think of any reason for her to haunt *me,* though, yet she's in that field whenever I pass by, coming or going. I've tried talking to her, but though she comes closer, she never speaks. It's worn me down. I've prayed and prayed, if not for her to move on, then at least for some clue about why she's always there! I've also turned to scripture for help!"

Here, Sam recited relevant passages from his pocket Bible, and the parson became assured that his talk of a ghost was sincere. Ruddle said he would like to join the young man at the field at some point, and Sam was overjoyed to find someone taking him seriously.

For now, the two went back to the house, where the Blighs quickly said they hoped Ruddle had talked some sense into the brat. This only sent their son running upstairs. When Ruddle then explained his plan to investigate the field, the others must have wondered what the point was of being so indulgent.

The next morning, Ruddle and Sam visited the haunted site, and sure enough, they spotted a specter in the shape of a woman there! Ruddle hid his astonishment and unease. The two saw the ghost again on their trip back, affirming that the ghost was *real!* Not only did the parson have to accept this himself—he also had to inform the Blighs of it. He did his best.

Making matters even more difficult, Ruddle had pressing obligations elsewhere. He promised to return after he had studied such ghostly phenomena. His absence grew even longer because his wife became sick, but the pastor continued to contemplate the case and do his research.

Finally, on July 27, he returned to Botathen and to the haunted field. After a while, he again encountered the ghost. His goal had been to speak to it, but it came no closer than ten feet. He spent the night at Botathen, where he managed to convince the parents and son to join him early the next morning for yet another ghost hunt.

That morning, with all three Blighs at his side, Ruddle spotted the ghost. He also made two interesting discoveries. A spaniel had tagged along on the walk, and it barked at and kept a distance from the ghost. This suggested that the spectral vision couldn't be attributed to the fear or the imagination of the witnesses. He also noticed that the ghost moved with an eerie, floating movement that suggested it wasn't someone perpetuating a hoax.

Of greater significance to Sam, his parents had witnessed the ghost. Their shocked expressions at doing so revealed as much, and afterward, they freely admitted it. They even acknowledged that, indeed, it was the spirit of Dorothy Dingly, whom they knew in life and whose funeral they had attended.

However, this was not the time for Ruddle to consult

with the spirit and find out why it wandered this field so persistently. He did that on his own the next morning, applying prayer, meditation, and the insights gained while researching such cases. It took a full day to coax the ghost into explaining itself, thereby paving the path for it to depart.

To be sure, Parson Ruddle succeeded in granting the ghost what it had wanted all along. It vanished quietly and was never seen again afterward.

Neither the 1720 nor the 1817 version reveals the reason for Dingly's ghostly return, which makes the tale end pretty disappointingly. Maybe the conversation between Ruddle and Dingly was protected by clergy–penitent privilege. Regardless, this finale makes this legend structurally very different from the tales of Athenodorus and Deshoulières. There is no "big reveal" at the conclusion, and this pushes the focus away from Ruddle solving the Dingly mystery and toward what came *before* it.

Why start with the funeral of John Eliott? This establishes a world troubled by the fact that even young people with promising futures die. Is there something beyond physical death? It's the age-old question, and certainly one familiar to ghost hunters because ghosts offer some kind of evidence that life continues in the Great Beyond. Whatever Dorothy Dingly's personal mission might have been, her returning from the dead makes that point.

But why is it important that Sam's parents—and even another clergyman—reject the boy's claim about the reality of ghosts? The Blighs are ultimately proven wrong to have spurned their son's testimony, but even Ruddle is careful and cautious in his acceptance of it. He questions the witness. He assesses Sam's character. He observes the phantom himself. He does his research, and he takes his time. Only then is he able to come fully to grips with the reality of a ghost and to coax it back to the unseen realm.

Much as Ruddle praises the deceased John Eliot for being a role model for other students, the legend presents Ruddle himself as an exemplar for those confronting the mystery of the afterlife. In other words, this is a parable about maintaining faith and, specifically, coupling faith with sound investigation.

The Problems of Putting a Legend on Paper

The publication history of Parson Ruddle's ghost story is complicated and confusing. Its debut before a general readership most likely came in an odd, 33-page pamphlet. The short narrative is titled "A Remarkable Passage of an Apparition, 1665," and it appears after a few unrelated poems. The pamphlet was released in 1720 and given the title *Mr. Campbell's Packet: for the Entertainment of Gentlemen and Ladies*, probably to take advantage of *The History of the Life and Adventures of Mr. Duncan Campbell,* an anonymous biography published the same year.

Decades later, William Lee suggested that the biography about Campbell *might* have been written by Daniel Defoe. With far greater confidence, he then attributes the pamphlet's ghost story to Defoe, but his evidence seems to be nothing more than his having written the somewhat similar "The Apparition of Mrs. Veal" (1706). (Worse still, it's not 100% certain that Defoe wrote the earlier ghost story.)[11] Another several decades passed before Robbins argued that, no, the author wasn't Defoe—it was Ruddle himself—as mentioned above. These matters are tough to settle.

Things became a bit messier in 1817, when Gilbert's version appeared. No author is theorized there, but along with details added here and there, this version introduces some minor changes. The parson's name is now spelled *Ruddell,* for instance, and Dorothy's surname is now

Dingley.[12] Nonetheless, it's close enough to the 1720 work overall to suppose that both rose from a common source or, perhaps, the earlier version was tweaked to form the later one.

Things got a *lot* messier in 1867, however, when yet another version was published with far more additions and alterations. This was written by Robert Stephen Hawker and titled "The Botathen Ghost." The parson's surname is now spelled *Rudall*, and Dorothy's is *Dinglet*. In addition, readers learn that the ghost-laying parson's diurnal—basically, a diary—"fell by chance into the hands of the present writer," but it's unclear if this refers to Hawker himself or to a narrator he invented. The basic plot points follow the 1720 and 1817 versions, but this "Rudall" wears a sanctified ring and hews a pentagram into the grass to protect himself from evil. This is a neat variation on the ropes and whips of other legendary Cornish ghost layers. In the earlier versions, the ghost's reason for returning to the land of the living is kept frustratingly vague. Hawker, though, reveals that Dorothy haunted the field in hopes of passing a message to Sam's father, encouraging him to atone for some past transgression.[13] There's a strong hint that something sinful happened between Mr. Bligh and Dorothy, making for a spicier tale.

Hawker's new version was first published in *All The Year Round*, a good magazine to find some great Victorian ghost stories, including Charles Dickens' "The Signal-Man" and Sheridan Le Fanu's "Madam Crowl's Ghost." Was "The Botathen Ghost" also a work of the imagination? An 1870 review suggests it probably was. For instance, the anonymous reviewer points out that the lines quoted from the diurnal "scarcely looks like English of the seventeenth century." In the late 1880s, A.H. Malan presented another case against the diurnal's authenticity, concluding that "there is sufficient internal evidence . . . to make it fairly certain that Mr. Ruddle could never have penned it." Instead,

Hawker found his inspiration in the 1720 version, "which he, at least, seems to have believed emanated directly from 'Parson Rudall.'"[14] Malan, a fellow clergyman, might have been too kind to make any stronger accusations against Hawker.

Yet some were believers, including another Victorian man of the cloth. In a fascinating article titled "Ghost-Layers and Ghost Laying," the Reverend R. Wilkins Rees declares his trust in Hawker's narrative and the claims about the diurnal therein. Describing it as "unquestionably the best account of all," Rees quotes the Hawker version at length because "the particulars it contains in connection with ghost-laying" provide insight into the practices of Anglican clergy two centuries earlier.[15] Did I mention that things got messier when the 1867 version appeared?

There's at least one more issue to ponder. The 1720, 1817, and 1867 versions all present Ruddle (or Ruddell or Rudall) as *telling his own story*. In other words, if Defoe wrote the first version, he pretended to be Ruddle himself chronicling the adventure—exactly what he had done a year earlier with the shipwrecked Robinson Crusoe. This is a called a first-person narrative.

However, legends are typically told in *third-person,* meaning the narrator is not a character or figure within the story. Instead, like an omniscient god, this narrator "floats above it," choosing whether or not to convey any characters' inner thoughts and private feelings. Pliny's account of the Athenodorus story and Couch's version of the Dodge adventure are examples of this. In my own rendition of the Ruddle tale presented above, I converted the earlier versions to a third-person narrative. I had a very easy time doing so, too, because it's such a plot-heavy piece. The perspective of one who was there isn't terribly necessary.

Can a *legend*—usually told a long time after the events and often presenting the characters as heroic or villainous in broad strokes—be told in the first-person? The simple answer is: sure, it can. It's more a technique of literature than folklore, though. Using a first-person narrator twists and complicates the feeling of realism in a story by prompting readers to picture a witness who was there at the time, and this is especially effective in a ghost story. Whoever wrote the 1720 version knew that a special quality is added to the story if it's presented as Ruddle's own record of the events. Hawker's introduction of the diurnal only raises this a notch or two.

Interestingly, using the first-person perspective also prompts the reader to wonder if the narrator is telling the story accurately. Is the storyteller especially biased or even delusional? What if the first-person narrator is an outright liar? If I'm right in interpreting this story to be ultimately about relying upon careful investigation to arrive at one's beliefs, then the first-person narration reinforces this idea nicely by nudging the discriminating reader to evaluate how much belief to grant the story being told.

This is something worth pondering in regard to the paranormal investigators to be discussed in the following chapters—the ghost hunters who are more historical than legendary. After all, we have first-person narrators in most of these cases.

---

[1] William Bottrell, *Traditions and Hearthside Stories of West Cornwall* (Printed for the Author by Beare and Son, 1873) pp. 124-25.

[2] Bottrell, p. 104. Flavell's death and parish are stated in *A Complete Parochial History of the County of Cornwall*, vol. 3 (William Lake, 1870) p. 385. His ghostly adventures can be found in R. Wilkins Rees' "Ghost-Layers and Ghost-Laying," *The Church Treasury of History, Custom, Folk-lore, etc.*, edited by William Andrews (William Andrews & Co., 1898) pp. 250-252.

[3] Thomas Bond, *Topographical and Historical Sketches of the Boroughs of East and West Looe, in the County of Cornwall* (Printed by J. Nichols and Son, 1823) pp. 154-155. Sadly, about fifty years after the

publication of Bond's book, the tombstone was described as "in fragments" in Jonathan Couch's *A History of Polperro, a Fishing Town on the South Coast of Cornwall* (W. Lake, 1871) p. 74.

[4] Thomas Q. Couch, "The Spectral Coach," *Popular Romances of the West of England; Or, The Drolls, Traditions, and Superstitions of Old Cornwall,* edited by Robert Hunt (John Camden Hotten, 1865) pp. 252-260. He claims to have heard it by fireside in an editorial note found in Jonathan Couch, p. 208.

[5] The Caistor Castle ghost is mentioned in John Gunn's "Proverbs, Adages and Popular Superstitions, Still Preserved in the Parish of Irstead," *Norfolk Archeology; or, Miscellaneous Tracts Relating to the Antiquities of the County of Norfolk,* vol. 2 (Charles Muskett, 1849) p. 306. The Blickling Hall ghost is mentioned in the footnotes of Henry Manship's *The History of Great Yarmouth,* edited by Charles John Palmer (Louis Alfred Meall, 1854) p. 207. Cuthbert Bede's article is "Old Supersitions, Part III: Carriage-and-Four Ghosts," *Illustrated London Magazine* 3 (November 1854) pp. 199-201.

[6] Francis Grose, *A Provincial Glossary* (Printed for S. Hooper, 1787) pp. 2-3 of the "Superstitions" section. Addison's report originally appeared in the July 6, 1711, issue of *The Spectator* and is reprinted in *The Spectator,* edited by Donald F. Bond, vol. 1 (Oxford at the Clarendon Press, 1965) p. 453.

[7] The *Glasgow Chronicle* article, dated January of 1826, is mentioned in Thomas Crofton Crocker's *Fairy Legends and Traditions of the South of Ireland,* vol. 2 (John Murray, 1828) p. 110. The Welsh specter is recorded in "Old Tales from West Wales VII: The Haunted Bridge," *The Red Dragon* 8 (1885) p. 267. The Irish beliefs come from Lageniensis [John O'Hanlon], *Legend Lays of Ireland* (John Mullany, 1870) p. 90.

[8] *A Handbook for Travellers on the Continent* (John Murray, 1838) p. 351. J. Hampden Porter, "Notes on the Folk-Lore of the Mountain Whites of the Alleghanies," *Journal of American Folklore* 7 (April-June 1894) p. 111. Washington Irving, "The Legend of Sleepy Hollow," *The Sketch Book of Geoffrey Crayon, Gent.,* vol. 6 (Printed by C.S. Van Winkle, 1820) pp. 51-117.

[9] Alfred F. Robbins, "A Cornish Ghost Story," *The Cornish Magazine* 1 (October 1898) pp. 283-297. S. Baring-Gould, *Cornish Characters and Strange Events* (John Lane, 1909) pp. 72-82.

[10] Robbins, p. 291.

[11] "A Remarkable Passage of an Apparition, 1665," *Mr. Campbell's Packet: for the Entertainment of Gentlemen and Ladies* (Printed for T. Bickerton, 1720) pp. 20-33. William Lee, *Daniel Defoe: His Life, and Recently Discovered Writings,* vol. 1 (John Camden Hotten, 1869) pp. 323-327. On the uncertainty of authorship of the 1706 tale, see George Starr, "Why Defoe Probably Did Not Write *The Apparition of Mrs. Veal,*" *Eighteenth Century Fiction* 15 (2003) pp. 421-450.

[12] C. S. Gilbert, *An Historical Survey of the County of Cornwall,* vol. 1 (J. Congdon, 1817) pp. 115-119.

[13] "The Botathen Ghost," *All the Year Round* 17 (May 18, 1867) pp. 501-504. Hawker's ending echoes a story told about Lord Lyttleton (1744-1779), in which he was haunted by "the figure of an unhappy female, whom he had seduced and abandoned, and who, when deserted, had put a violent end to her own existence." The ghost announces Lyttleton will die in three days and bids him to repent his sins. Whether or not he repented, he died on schedule. See Clarence Day, *Remarkable Apparitions and Ghost-Stories* (Wilson and Company, 1848) pp. 36-37.

[14] Charles Dickens, "The Signal-Man," *All the Year Round,* Christmas number (December 10, 1866) pp. 20-25. Sheridan Le Fanu, "Madam Crowl's Ghost," *All the Year Round* 5.109 (December 31, 1870) pp. 114-120. "Mr. Hawker's 'Footprints of Former Men in Far Cornwall.'" *Spectator* 43 (October 29, 1870) p. 1290. A.H. Malan's "Some Remarks on Parson Rudall and the Botathen Ghost," *Transactions of the Penzance Natural History and Antiquarian Society* 3 (1888-89) p. 61.

[15] Rees, p. 242.

PART TWO

HISTORICAL
GHOST HUNTS

CHAPTER THREE

THE RELIABILITY OF EVIDENCE: JOSEPH GLANVILL AND THE MOMPESSON HAUNTING

Joseph Glanvill (1636-1680) has a vital place in the history of—if not ghost hunting specifically—then paranormal investigation in general. Three centuries after he lived, two prominent figures in the study of supernatural and occult topics named Glanvill as the founder of the kind of work they were both doing. Of the pair, Harry Price was more likely found "out in the field," debunking mediums or snooping around haunted houses. He wrote that "Glanvill can be regarded as the Father of Psychical Research," this being a term for paranormal study. In contrast, Montague Summers probably spent more of his time paging through timeworn books, preparing to write his popular histories of witchcraft, vampires, and werewolves. Nonetheless, Summers agrees with Price: "There is no more important figure in the history of English psychical research than Joseph Glanvil."[1] (Whether the surname ought to be spelled "Glanvill" or "Glanvil" remains undecided.) Both Price and Summers apparently traced their own work to a single ancestor.

Glanvill served in the Anglican Church in the west of England, close to where he was born and not terribly far from those legendary parsons who contended with ghosts and devils down in Cornwall. At one point, Glanvill acted as chaplain to King Charles II (1630-1685), an achievement probably won because of the clergyman's prominence as an astute intellectual. Among Glanvill's writings, *Sadducismus Triumphatus; or, Full and Plain Evidence Concerning Witches and Apparitions* stands out. Published a year after his death, it was an expanded version of an earlier book, probably augmented by a colleague named Henry More. *Sadducismus Triumphatus* presents an argument in favor of the reality of apparitions—and, as the title makes clear, in favor of the reality of witchcraft. It is a tragic fact that the history of ghost hunting became tangled with the history of witch hunting. In fact, Glanvill's book could well have influenced people who supported the executions and other punishments inflicted upon those accused of witchcraft in places as far away from England as Salem, Massachusetts.[2]

After a section exploring the theoretical *possibility* of witches and ghosts, *Sadducismus Triumphatus* turns to a series of "relations," meaning specific *reports* of them. The first relation concerns weird manifestations in the house of the Mompesson family, and this became the book's most famous case. It's also a case that Glanvill investigated personally. Unlike the Parson Ruddle documents, it's generally agreed that Glanvill himself chronicled this ghost hunt, and I summarize, paraphrase, and modernize the story below from that document. Again, I use the third-person, making this something like a police report based on Glanvill's testimony.[3]

John Mompesson was a magistrate from Tidworth, Wiltshire, England. In March of 1661, he was visiting an acquaintance who worked as the bailiff for the nearby village of Ludgershall.[4] Upon hearing someone beating a drum outside, Mompesson asked his host if there was some reason for the noise. The bailiff explained that, for several days, a beggar was banging the drum to solicit money—something like a busker, but far more annoying. Assuming Mompesson understood that the beggar would require a certified pass to do what he was doing, the bailiff added that he *had* made sure the legal paperwork was at hand. However, he also suspected it might be counterfeit.

Mompesson took charge. He had the beggar brought before him. Checking the certification himself, the magistrate saw that the signatures were those of Sir William Cawley and Colonel Ayliff of Gretenham. Mompesson knew these men and, in fact, knew them well enough to recognize these signatures *weren't* done in their handwriting! He ordered the beggar to be taken before the Justice of the Peace and the bothersome drum to be confiscated

About a month later, the beggar had been let free. The drum had found its way to Mompesson's home back in Tidworth. This is when things became strange. Mompesson returned from another trip, this one to London, and learned from his wife that there had been disturbing noises. It had sounded like thieves in the night or as if the house itself were cracking. That night, Mompesson heard loud knocks on the doors, and upon investigating with a couple of pistols ready, he heard more knocks in other spots. He couldn't find any explanation. When he went back to bed, more noises—thumping and *drumming*—came from the roof above him.

The noises continued for months, usually starting whenever the Mompessons went to bed and ending a couple of hours or so afterward. Gradually, the drumming had drifted from outside the house to inside it, specifically, to the very room where the beggar's drum had been stored. Still, no explanation was found.

And yet there seemed to be an awareness or a consciousness lurking behind the weird phenomenon.

As mentioned, it began *whenever* the Mompessons went to bed, whether it was early or late. At one point, Mrs. Mompesson became bedridden, and then the drumming stopped, as if politely allowing her to rest. After that, however, it grew ruder. It targeted the youngest children, pounding their bedsteads violently. It began beating recognizable rhythms from well-known military songs.

Then came the scratching. It was heard under the children's beds and sounded like it was made by iron claws. Those beds would even be lifted into the air! The parents tried having the children sleep in a loft at the top of the house, but the disembodied pest followed and harassed them there, too.

On November 5, 1661, the Mompessons made a key discovery: the entity could be provoked to perform. A courageous servant was in the children's room and noticed two boards seeming to move by themselves. He bid the entity, for lack of a better term, to bring him one of the boards. Indeed, the invisible hand moved one of the boards to within a yard or so. "No," said the servant, "let me have it *in my hand.*" The entity not only complied—it moved the board up and down, left and right, continuing to do so until Mr. Mompesson forbid the servant from ever again inciting such a display. There were several witnesses to this, and afterward, the room reeked of *sulfur.* In other words, there was a whiff of the Devil's work being done.

That very night, a minister named Mr. Cragg visited the house. A knocking then started very loudly at the children's bedside, and Cragg led prayers at the spot. The noises moved to the attic room. Once the prayers ended—in full sight of everyone there—the chairs began to "walk" by themselves! The entity next hurled the children's shoes over the heads of those watching, and it moved other loose objects, too. A bedstaff—

which is a wooden pin, about the length of a rolling pin, used to hold the linens in place—was tossed at the minister. Eerily, the pin fell softly and did no harm to the man.

Mompesson knew he must protect his children. He arranged for them to stay with neighbors, all except the eldest daughter. She was moved to the parents' room, but the ten-year-old girl was still pestered there by drumming and other noises. This went on for three weeks. In that time, another key discovery was made: rudimentary communication with the entity could be made! If someone drummed a particular pattern, the entity would repeat it. At one point, several people were gathered to observe the manifestations, and a gentleman called out, "Satan, if this drummer summoned you forth to harass this house, give three knocks and no more." Three knocks sounded—and no more! For confirmation, the gentleman asked, "If you are the drummer, give five knocks and no more tonight." Five knocks were heard, and the rest of the night was quiet.

The manifestations continued for several more months. Others visited the house and attested to experiencing otherworldly phenomena. There wasn't much visual evidence of the entity other than blue lights floating around the house. There was much more proof that the thing could move physical objects. It threw clothes around and pulled blankets off of those sleeping. Doors opened and closed by themselves. It hid a Bible in the fireplace ashes, and it even lifted people off their beds.

Mostly, the entity made itself *heard.* Along with those knocks and the drumming, disembodied singing came from the chimney. Inexplicable footsteps—not just of *one* entity but of *several*—were heard. At one point, the thing panted like an exhausted dog.

Mompesson said he had heard a rustling of silky cloth, too, and an overnight guest affirmed this, adding that he had to struggle against the entity to reach his sword in response to the noise. Perhaps the most disturbing sound came one morning, when something banged near the children. As Mompesson rushed to them, he and the children heard a voice that cried, *"A witch! A witch!"*

After reports about the haunting had spread and persisted, Glanvill arrived in Tidworth to investigate. His first task was to verify with neighbors what he had learned from potentially unreliable sources. Next, he met with witnesses—two ministers among them—at the Mompesson house. Only one gentleman had remained with Glanvill and Mompesson by 8:00 p.m., when a maid came to inform them that the entity was manifesting in the children's room. Glanvill was still climbing the stairs when he heard the strange scratching. He tracked it to behind a headboard in the children's room. Two girls, aged about seven or eight years, shared this bed, and their hands were in clear view above the bedding, confirming that they weren't making the noise. (By the time of Glanvill's investigation, the girls had grown accustomed to such disturbances.)

Glanvill felt behind the mattress at the spot where the scratching seemed to come. The noise moved to another spot, but it returned as soon he stopped. He experimented with something he had learned about the entity. He scratched the sheet a certain number of times—five scratches, seven scratches, ten scratches—and each time, the entity repeated the same number. He peered under the bed, searched behind it, looked under the bedding, tested the bedframe, tapped on the wall beside it, and investigated everything else he could think to investigate. One of his companions did the same, but neither one uncovered any trick, contrivance, or physical cause to explain the noise.

At this point, Glanvill became convinced he was dealing with the supernatural, be it demon or spirit. Meanwhile, the scratching continued for about half an hour, moving around under the bed. It then began to make the loud panting sound—so loud, in fact, that the windows vibrated. Again, the men searched, this time expecting to find a dog, a cat, or some other animal. Nothing.

And then Glanvill's eye caught a sudden movement. Something had wriggled. It was a linen bag hanging against another bed. No one was near it, but what if a mouse or a rat had gotten caught in this bag? It wouldn't explain the panting, but it was certainly worth inspecting. He swiftly lifted the bag and carefully ran it through his free hand. Again, nothing.

Unable to attribute the scratching, the panting, or the wriggling to any natural cause, Glanvill finally retired. As previously arranged, he would spend the rest of the night in the room where the disturbances had originated. He slept well for the most part. Shortly before sunrise, though, he awoke to a loud knocking. Repeatedly, he asked who was there, but the only answer was more knocking.

At last, he shouted, "In the name of God, who is it, and what do you want?"

A voice answered, "Nothing with you."

Subsequent questioning of Mompesson and the servants confirmed that no one would have been in that part of the house at that time.

Glanvill's narrative of his investigation ends with an anecdote that he admits might be coincidence—but an *odd* coincidence, given what had come before. His horse had been in good health on the trip to Tidworth. It was provided a clean stable and good food there.

However, on the morning of the return trip, the horse was found sweating. The poor creature fell lame during the easy journey home, and it died two or three days afterward. No one was able to explain it.

Glanvill continues the "relation" with additional incidents that occurred in the Mompesson house after he had left. These involve cruel pranks the entity played on the family, especially the children, and their guests. It would make an excellent story of a vengeful ghost, if the beggar whose drum Mompesson had confiscated were found to have died shortly before the manifestations started. But no. The beggar was alive. In fact, he had been in prison for theft much of the time when the Mompessons were plagued by the entity. In other words, it's doubtful he was somehow playing an elaborate trick.

Instead of a tale of ghostly revenge, Glanvill's narrative has been classified as an early record of poltergeist activity by prominent ghostologists. Catherine Crowe mentions the case in a chapter titled "The Poltergeist of the Germans, and Possession" in her influential book *The Night Side of Nature; or, Ghosts and Ghost Seers,* first published in 1848. Price's comment about Glanvill being the father of psychical research is in his book devoted to poltergeist phenomena, where the Mompesson haunting is given a complete chapter.[5]

Glanvill himself, on the other hand, wants his readers to see the Tidworth incidents as evidence of vengeful witchcraft. This becomes apparent when he concludes the report by saying that the beggar, while in prison, claimed responsibility for the supernatural harassment of the Mompessons, all in retaliation for not returning his drum. It was a very unwise boast in an age when witchcraft was still a punishable crime. The beggar was promptly tried as a witch. Evidence from and witnesses of the Mompesson haunting were introduced at his trial, and the beggar was found guilty.

Rather than being condemned to execution or some form of torture, the beggar was sentenced with transportation, meaning exile from the country. Glanvill ends this part of *Sadducismus Triumphatus* with a flourish that some might consider farfetched. He says that the powerful conjurer managed—perhaps by raising storms—to bring the ship on which he was to be deported back into harbor. Glanvill adds that, in earlier days, the beggar often spoke about possessing important books that had once belonged to someone reputed to be a wizard.

Exactly how Glanvill had learned all of this about the beggar is left unstated. Readers are left to wonder why such a gifted witch had become reduced to beating a drum to solicit charity.

Glanvill Was Participating in a Debate

One thing I've learned about history is that it's often a mistake to ask: "What did people believe back then?" The better question is: "What did people *disagree about* back then?" After all, any large group of human beings rarely agrees on anything. Whether it's a strength or a weakness— or a blend of both—we certainly seem to be an argumentative species. The topic of ghosts illustrates this particularly well. Remember that, when Pliny recorded the legend about Athenodorus, he wanted to know if Sura found it convincing. That was two millennia ago, and even then, people didn't all agree that ghosts were real.

The first sign that Glanvill was writing to convince his readers that witches and apparitions are real appears in the title: *Sadducismus Triumphatus*. Roughly translated, this means "a triumph over Sadducism." This is similar to the title of Glanvill's earlier work: "A Blow at Modern Sadducism in Some Considerations about Witchcraft" (1668), in which he also discusses the Mompesson haunting.

Sadducism refers to an ancient sect of Judaism that rejected some of the most cherished tenets of that faith, including an afterlife and the existence of angels. The New Testament mentions that Jesus warned his followers against falling for the doctrines of the Sadducees.[6] (Did I mention that human beings sure like to disagree?) Given that Glanvill was an Anglican clergyman, it's unsurprising that he aligned himself with Christ in this way.

However, his opposition was not Sadducism in a literal sense. In the 1600s, various schools of thought challenged traditional views of the supernatural. Glanvill was born only two years before Antoinette du Ligier de la Garde Deshoulières. As explained in Chapter One, this poet's philosophy held that natural causes underlie phenomena frequently mistaken to be supernatural. While such materialists debunked ghosts and witchcraft, a group called the deists spread the idea that, while a Supreme Creator did indeed exist, Divine Intervention did not. Instead, God remained at a distance, and interaction between the supernatural and natural worlds—including miracles, prophesies, even revelation from above—were all matters of superstition. According to deism, God's greatest gift to humanity was our ability to think reasonably and to discover proof of the Grand Designer in the natural world. In other words, to find God, look to what Galileo gleaned from the solar system and what Newton observed in physical laws here on Earth instead of in centuries-old scripture or in alleged spectral manifestations.

That Glanvill knows there are skeptics among his readers is also made clear in the first part of *Sadducismus Triumphatus*. There, he raises a series of objections to the reality of witches and apparitions before responding to them. For instance, the second objection involves feats witches are said to have accomplished, which "are ridiculous and impossible in the nature of things." Flying through the air, turning into cats, and reciting certain incantations to raise storms are among these hard-to-swallow tricks. Glanvill summarizes this position and next presents his counter-argument. Essentially, he claims that the weirder the report, the more he's inclined to believe it. Someone deliberately fabricating a story, after all, keeps it as close to "unsuspected realities" as possible—otherwise, such a person will be judged as "a fool or a mad man." There's also too much consistency in the reports about witches to deem them purely flights of fancy, since the imagination creates "the most various things in all the world." Besides, witches don't do these things themselves. They depend upon "the agency of those wicked *confederates* they employ," and all we know about these beings is that they exist beyond the confines of earthly physics.[7] In this way, Glanvill reminds readers to see the topic as part of a dialog and to avoid automatically accepting his convictions as the final word.

This "tennis-game" technique of making an argument by refuting of series of opposing claims was certainly not unique. In fact, an earlier—and much more infamous—book about witchcraft uses the same strategy. Written by Matthew Hopkins, the self-styled "Witch Finder Generall," *The Discovery of Witches* (1647) presents the author's defense of his extraordinary record of identifying witches and of his cruel and illegal methods to coerce confessions. One of the "inquiries" that Hopkins answers concerns "an abominable, inhumane, and unmerciful trial of these poor [accused] creatures, by tying them and heaving them into the water, a trial not allowable by law or conscience." In reply, Hopkins says the victims agree to the test, called "ducking." When witches agree to it, they are confident the Devil will protect them. He also explains the rationale of ducking: having made a pact with Satan, witches deny their baptisms, and so the water rejects them and "suffers them to float."[8] Both Glanvill and Hopkins knew that witchcraft was controversial, and their respective writing acknowledges this (though Hopkins might well have been insisting that his zealous actions were *not* downright criminal and/or deplorable).

Glanvill reveals his awareness of doubting readers in another way, too. As he recounts his investigation in the "Evidence" section of the book, he addresses those who would dismiss what he heard and saw as products of fear rather than anything supernatural. He writes:

> It will I know be said by some that my friend and I were under some affright, and so fancied noises and sights that were not [real]. . . . But if it is possible to know how a man is affected when in fear and when unconcerned, I certainly know for my own part that, during the whole time of my being in that room and in the house, I was under no more affrightment than I am while I write this relation. And if I know that I am now awake and that I see objects that are before me, I know that I heard and saw the particulars I have told.[9]

Of course, this is a bit like saying "trust me because I'm trustworthy," but it's interesting that Glanvill openly considered alternative explanations to what he witnessed. Even after doing so, he remained convinced that something supernatural was happening at the Mompessons' house.

In this way, Glanvill hoped to use reports of paranormal activity to push against what he perceived as mounting skepticism. Others followed. In *The History of Apparitions, Ghosts, Spirits or Spectres* (1762) the author—identified only as "a CLERGYMAN"—explains: "However atheists, deists, and free-thinkers may ridicule the notion of ghosts and apparitions, every true believer of the Christian religion cannot doubt the reality of such appearances." In *A Relation of Apparitions of Spirits in the Principality of Wales* (1780), the minister Edmund Jones explains that this collection of true ghost stories is intended to quell the spreading "denial of the being of spirits and apparitions, which has a tendency to irreligion and atheism, for when men come to deny the being of spirits, the next step is to deny the being of God, who is a spirit and the Father of Spirits." [10]

The fear that religious faith was crumbling persisted for a full century (and, no doubt, well afterward). In *The Other World; or, Glimpses of the Supernatural,* published in 1875, the Reverend Frederick George Lee explains why he's sharing his collection of reports about such phenomena as omens, miracles, ghosts, wraiths, and witchcraft. (The inclusion of witchcraft is remarkable, given how belief in it had virtually disappeared by the end of the 1700s.) Lee says that God grants humanity such "examples of supernatural intervention" to confirm the existence of the Great Beyond, that ethereal realm "in which the sceptic and the materialist of the present restless age would have us disbelieve, and which they themselves scornfully reject." [11]

I won't say that Glanvill *led* the charge of clergyman who used chronicles of supernatural encounters as a weapon against atheism, deism, and other views that cast doubt on supernatural events occurring in the natural world. Another lesson about history that I've learned is to be very careful when claiming something is a first—after all, I haven't read *everything.* However, I can confidently say that Glanvill wasn't the *last* to use this strategy of debate.

Carefully Weighing the Evidence

It's a mistake to attribute the witch hunts of the 1600s solely to a tidal wave of panic and religious fervor. Odd though it might seem, some writers of that century managed to balance the persecution of witches with critical thinking. By "critical" here, I mean being mindful of the reliability of the evidence and of the logic underlying conclusions drawn from that evidence. Long before Glanvill investigated the Mompesson house, other authors had written about how to best identify and try witches. It's worth looking at a couple of these works to better understand Glanvill's concern for the reliability of his evidence.

We start with *Daemonlogie* (1597), by King James, the same man who commissioned a version of the Bible that remains in use. This book, by so notable an author, had an understandable impact on how British authors portrayed witches through the 1600s. For example, it's been said that *Daemonlogie* influenced Shakespeare's play *Macbeth*, which debuted around 1606, and Witch Finder Generall Hopkins refers directly to it in his 1647 book. An interesting element of James's book, though, is that it is not just about how to test those accused for witchcraft. It also advises investigators to consider if *accusers* have misinterpreted phenomena explainable in other ways—and to be on guard for downright fakery. James had been personally involved with at least one case of a victim confessing to having faked evidence of bewitchment, and he very likely knew of other similar ones. According to historian Elizabeth Mack, this led the king to emphasize in his book the "necessity to investigate the guilt of the person accused and to also assess the legitimacy of the victim's claims."[12] In essence, James encouraged paranormal investigators to balance supernatural explanations against natural ones.

The idea that there might be alternative explanations to what *seems* like witchcraft also appears in Richard Bernard's *A Guide to Grand-Jury Men* (1630). In the second chapter, Bernard says that perfectly natural causes—especially medical conditions—can be at work. Catalepsy and apoplexy explain sudden trance-like states, and Bernard cites medical experts and specific cases. He does the same to explain seizures, illustrating his point with "a poor boy of Pytchley in Northamptonshire" who suddenly suffered from violent convulsions. The boy's parents first "sent for a wise woman, who played her witchery tricks, but could do nothing." Next, a physician was brought in, and the boy was diagnosed with a worm infection. He became healthy again once the worms were eradicated. Bernard ends the chapter by encouraging those overseeing witch trials to consult medical doctors before making any final rulings.

In the very next chapter, Bernard explores trials in which those who accused others of witchcraft were themselves committing fraud. "Did not our late King James, by his wisdom, learning, and experience, uncover diverse counterfeits?" asks the author. This chapter follows a pattern similar to the previous one, summarizing a variety of cases that proved to be fraudulent. To explain why people pretend to be afflicted by witchcraft, Bernard provides a list that includes gain, vengeance, and the urge simply to trick others. He then advises those in charge of witch trials to carefully "look upon the seemingly bewitched and to ponder all the circumstances, lest they be deceived by a counterfeit."[13] Those prosecuting witches, then, were advised to consider if the case could be debunked, a guard against fanaticism.

And we see this kind of caution applied in Glanvill's investigation of the Mompesson haunting. First, Glanvill explains how he assessed the testimony of Mompesson, his chief eyewitness to the paranormal manifestations. He says, "Now, the credit of matters of fact depends much upon those who relate them, who, if they cannot be deceived themselves nor supposed any ways interested to impose upon others, ought to be credited." In other words, Glanvill considered if Mompesson had been fooled himself or had been trying to fool others. But the magistrate was too smart to mistake the *abundance* of weird phenomena occurring in his house over the course of *years*. If his servants had been deceiving him, he would have caught them. The same holds with his family, who were hardly likely to be motivated to continue any such pranks for such a long time. If some psychological condition had made Mompesson delusional, how could that ailment have "infected his whole family and those multitudes of neighbors, who had so often been witnesses" to the same delusions? In the end, Glanvill judges his key witness to be reliable.

Those many *other* witnesses are also among Glanvill's concerns. He assesses this body of evidence as a whole, again deeming it reliable because these remarkable manifestations did not happen

> long ago or at far distance, in an ignorant age, or among a barbarous people. They were not seen by only two or three [psychologically troubled] and/or superstitious people, and reported by those who made them serve the advantage and interest of a party. They were not the events of a day or night, nor the vanishing glances of an apparition. Indeed, these manifestations were near and late, public, frequent, and of several years' continuance, witnessed by multitudes of competent and unbiased attesters, and acted in a searching, incredulous age.

Current. Local. Abundant. Persistent. Witnessed by trust-worthy people in an era when it's tough to believe in such things. Glanvill deems his body of evidence to be, in a word, reliable.

He even addresses the possibility that his *own* experiences at the Mompesson house might be, if not flawed, then suspect. In earlier chronicles, Glanvill left out some of his experiences found in *Sadducismus Triumphatus.* For instance, one addition is the fact he saw the linen bag wriggling and found no rodent or anything else alive inside. He explains that he had kept this out of his previous narrations "because it depended on my testimony alone," but intelligent men had convinced him to include it. Likewise, Glanvill had worried about mentioning the knocking and unaccountable voice heard in the early morning after sleeping in the room where the manifestations had begun. They were, he says, "not such plain and unexceptional proofs."[14] He seems to be saying that, as with his horse going lame, there are other possible explanations that don't involve the supernatural. Why did Glanvill decide to include these parts of his investigation if he had thought them dodgy before? He might have been persuaded by others to do so, or he might have felt that—given all the other freaky events at the Mompessons' house—these could well have been more of the same. If nothing else, those details certainly make his investigation report a bit more intriguing and memorable.

It's true that Glanvill was inconsistent in his concern for trustworthy evidence. That stuff about the beggar once boasting about having had access to books on wizardry and then possibly raising storms to stay in England certainly smacks of grand storytelling. Given his diligence in scrutinizing his sources elsewhere, though, Glanvill himself probably wasn't the original storyteller. Maybe he just heard something that fit so nicely with his view on witchcraft that he fell under its spell.

Given his firm conviction that witchcraft was real, isn't Glanvill better labeled a witch hunter—or, perhaps, a psychical researcher—than a *ghost* hunter? My answer is obvious, since I've included him in this book. In my defense, Glanvill followed the nocturnal surveillance tradition of Athenodorus and exhibited a dash of Deshoulières in his consideration of alternative natural explanations. Yet neither these philosophers—nor Parsons Dodge and Ruddle— showed quite the same concern as Glanvill for weighing the reliability of witness testimony. While that might be one of the differences between legend and history, it's here that Glanvill's account of his investigation of the Mompesson haunting provides a valuable model for the generations of ghost hunters who followed.

----

[1] Harry Price, *Poltergeist Over England: Three Centuries of Mischievous Ghosts* (Country Life Ltd., 1945) pp. 62-63. Montague Summers, Introduction to *Pandæmonium,* by Richard Bovet (Hands and Flower, 1951) p. xi.

[2] E. William Monter posits a likely connection between Glanvill's book and Cotton Mather's later defense of the Salem witch trials in *The Wonders of the Invisible World.* Both works present a case of children alleged to be bewitched in Dalarna, Sweden, as evidence for the reality of witchcraft. See Monter's "Scandinavian Witchcraft in Anglo-American Perspective," *Early Modern European Witchcraft: Centres and Peripheries,* edited by Bengt Ankarloo and Gustav Henningsen (Clarendon, 1990) p. 432.

[3] Glanvill revised his account of the Mompesson haunting over time, and I adapted this from the version found in his *Sadducismus Triumphatus; Or, Full and Plain Evidence Concerning Witches and Apparitions* (Printed for A.L., 1700) pp. 49-62 of the "Evidence" section.

[4] I'm using the town names found on current maps. Glanvill calls these towns "Tedworth" and "Ludgarshal."

[5] Catherine Crowe, *The Night Side of Nature; Or, Ghosts and Ghost Seers,* vol. 2 (T.C. Newby, 1848) p. 268. Price, pp. 43-61.

[6] Matthew 16:12 KJV.

[7] Glanvill, pp. 6-7 of the "Some Considerations Concerning Witchcraft" section.

[8] Matthew Hopkins, *The Discovery of Witches* (H.W. Hunt, 1931) pp. 5-6. This is a facsimile of the 1647 work.

[9] Glanvill, p. 56 of the "Evidence" section.

[10] *The History of Apparitions, Ghosts, Spirits and Spectres* (Printed for J. Simpson, 1762) p. iv. Edmund Jones, *A Relation of Apparitions and Spirits* (NA, 1780) pp. iii. Jones is confirmed as this anonymous work's author in Jonathan Barry's "News from the Invisible World: The Publishing History of Tales of the Supernatural," *Cultures of Witchcraft in Europe from the Middle Ages to the Present* (Palgrave Macmillan, 2018) p. 200.

[11] Frederick George Lee, *The Other World; Or, Glimpses of the Supernatural,* vol. 1 (Henry S. King, 1875) p. 7.

[12] For a detailed discussion of James's influence on Shakespeare, see Henry Paul's *The Royal Play of Macbeth: When, Why, and How It Was Written* (Macmillan, 1950). Hopkins, p. 6. Elizabeth Mack, "The *Malleus Maleficarum* and King James: Defining Witchcraft," *Voces Novae* 1.1 (2009) p. 195.

[13] Richard Bernard, *A Guide to Grand-Jury Men* (Printed by Felix Kyngston, 1630) pp. 18, 34, 38-39.

[14] Glanvill, pp. 60, 62, 56-57 of the "Evidence" section.

CHAPTER FOUR

THE INVESTIGATIVE TEAM: ALDRICH, JOHNSON, AND THE COCK LANE CASE

A catchier title for this chapter might be "The Ghostly Revenge of William Kent's Lovers" or maybe "The Scratching Spectral Sisters." But this would be misleading because any and all ghosts involved in the Cock Lane case were deemed to be a hoax. "If one phantom is more discredited than another, it is the Cock Lane ghost," says Andrew Lang in *Cock Lane and Common-sense,* in which he attempts to give paranormal phenomena a fair and balanced trial.[1] Still, any and all ghost hunters can benefit from knowing about the events happening on Cock Lane in London in the late 1750s and early 1760s. It remains one of the most famous paranormal investigations in England and beyond.

Unfortunately, the story is a complex one, and the sequence of events grows murky at times. Questions are left open. Using a sort of Morse code, the alleged ghost eventually identified itself as the spirit of Frances Lynes— but this woman was still alive when the first manifestations occurred. Were there *two* ghosts, then, who traded places? These ghosts supposedly terrified the Parsons residence over the course of about two years. Why did it take so long for Parsons go public with it? Once communication was established, the ghost of Lynes accused William Kent of having *murdered* her. Some concluded it was a hoax created by Parsons, an act inflamed by a lawsuit with Kent—but why such an *elaborate* scheme for revenge? It was a very public and popular case, so to what extent were witness reports sensationalized to sell newspapers? Making matters more aggravating, subsequent writers have retold the history inconsistently, at times, going so far as introducing different names for the key figures.[2]

I'll do my best to sort out the story by drawing from historical documents written as the events were unraveling. These are certainly not guaranteed to be accurate—in fact, in spots, they are inconsistent with one another—but they're historically close to the actual events. This, then, might be the story as it was pieced together by readers in the early 1760s.

The Case

Elizabeth Kent was dead. She had died giving birth to a son, who also passed away a short time later. Through the ordeal, Elizabeth was cared for by her sister, Frances Lynes. This kind woman, known and remembered as Fanny, then consoled the distraught husband and father, William Kent. Even after the arrangements for and affairs of her sister and nephew were settled, Lynes lingered at Kent's house in Norfolk.

As they sometimes do, a loving attachment rose between Kent and his sister-in-law. A sexual under-standing emerged, too. Was it what we now term a co-dependent relationship? Whether it was a healthy situation or not, it would have been sternly frowned upon by many of their neighbors. In fact, the prospect of marriage between the two was illegal. Two centuries earlier, the Church of England had formalized a "Table of Kindred and Affinity, Wherein Whosoever Are

Related are Forbidden in Scripture and Our Laws to Marry Together," and this made clear that a man was banned from marrying his sister-in-law and a woman from marrying her brother-in-law.[3] That ban was so firmly entrenched that it remained in place until 1907. Maybe Lynes could have passed as Kent's housekeeper, but that possibility was foiled by a new development. There was a pregnancy.[4] What was the couple to do? Kent moved to London, and after some struggle to remain apart, Lynes joined him. They posed as a married couple while seeking temporary lodgings before settling in at someplace more permanent. This would have been around 1759, and at this point, dates become important.

They found a room to let in a house on Cock Lane. Their new landlord was Richard Parsons, who served as the parish clerk of what is now called Holy Sepulchre Church. Though taking in boarders was fairly typical, Parsons' occupation wasn't a well-paying one, and at some point, he borrowed money from Kent. Forgive the pun, but the difficulty in repaying this debt would come to *haunt* Parsons.

Meanwhile, the Parsons' eleven- or twelve-year-old daughter Elizabeth seemed to be at the center of her own haunting. She would later say that, on a night when Kent was away and she was sharing a bed with the pregnant Lynes, the two heard weird scratching and knocks. At first, it was attributed to a nearby cobbler, but he didn't work on Sundays—apparently, the spirit did. Parsons' wife and some of their neighbors confirmed the inexplicable sounds.

However, the reports of this first visitation were made in *1762*.

Back in 1760, Kent and Lynes left Cock Lane for an apartment in nearby Barlett Court. Parsons still hadn't repaid his debt. No doubt, sharing a house would have been difficult, and though it's hard to say that this is why Kent had found new lodgings, it *is* known that he sued Parsons for that money at some point. As if that wasn't enough, in their new residence, Lynes grew very sick. She was still pregnant when she died of smallpox. The death occurred on February 2 of that same year.[5]

In January of 1762, close to two years after Fanny Lynes' death, more paranormal activity was reported at the Cock Lane house. Again, young Elizabeth always seemed to be present for the knocking and scratching, as if she were the medium the spirit depended on to manifest in the physical world. Of course, this remounting of ghostly activity began *before* it appeared in the press, but *London Magazine* still figures that "the space of above a year and a half" passed between the time Lynes and little Elizabeth were bothered in their bed and the "second visitation." [6]

In contrast, that month's issues of *Gentleman's Magazine* and *Universal Magazine* each say the manifestations had been present the whole two years. If the Parsons' house had been continuously haunted for two years, one is likely to ask for clarification. First, did Parsons let his family endure the haunting all that time before soliciting help or, at least, engaging outside witnesses? Reportedly—and again, this is the story told at the start of 1762—he had the walls checked. That only increased the disturbances. He also had Elizabeth moved to a different room in the house, but the noise-maker followed her there.[7] Exactly when these alleged attempts to deal with the haunting occurred is vague, and it still seems like a minimal effort to rid one's family of a two-year unwanted supernatural house-mate.

Another question is whose ghost was it? The three magazines mentioned above all agree that, by 1762, the ghost identified itself as Fanny Lynes. You see, a system of communication had been devised: one knock for yes and two knocks for no. But why had Lynes' spirit taken so long—about two years—to travel the short distance from her deathbed on Barlett Court to Cock Lane? Perhaps, time and space work differently in the spirit realm.

There's more, though. If the first wave of activity had happened when Lynes was still alive, whose ghost had caused it? Well, in 1762, little Elizabeth Parsons attributed that first visitation to Elizabeth Kent, née Lynes. Do some more math, and we find there's a lapse of about two or three years between *that* woman's death and her posthumous attempt to communicate with Fanny Lynes and the girl. The Lynes sisters seem to have made rather sluggish spirits.[8] And at what point did Elizabeth Kent pass the knocking baton to Fanny Lynes?

These puzzles hardly mattered when compared to the prospect of *a ghost with communication skills* at Cock Lane! Granted, its knocks restricted the phantom to little more than yes and no answers, but a lot of information could still be gleaned this way. To be sure, some very startling information was ascertained! As mentioned, this was how the ghost was identified as Frances Lynes. This was also how the ghost's purpose for lingering in the material world was discovered. Reminiscent of Dorothy Dingly in Launceton, Fanny Lynes returned from the dead to reveal a secret.

Unlike the one in Launceton, though, the Cock Lane ghost's message was not kept confidential. Indeed, it was publically proclaimed: Lynes had been *murdered!* Yes, she had been *poisoned,* and the fiend responsible was *William Kent!*

The Investigations

Imagine the sensation! Not only was there a ghost! This ghost—this chatty phantom—had accused her illicit lover of murdering her! As soon as the news broke, the Parsons' residence was besieged. One of the gawkers was author Horace Walpole, who described the scene in a letter dated February 2, 1762. He and a party of aristocrats had attended the opera, followed by a jaunt to Cock Lane:

> [I]t rained torrents; yet the lane was full of mob, and the house so full we could not get in. At last they discovered it was the Duke of York, and the company squeezed themselves into one another's pockets to make room for us. . . . When we opened the chamber, in which were fifty people with no light, but one tallow candle at the end, we tumbled over the bed of the child to whom the ghost comes, and whom they are murdering by inches in such insufferable heat and stench.[9]

It seems young Elizabeth, the medium through which the ghost communicated, was being exploited like a child star in Hollywood.

Mistreatment of a minor, though, wasn't the inspiration for a series of investigations that were soon organized. Instead, they were launched to test the authenticity of the haunting. One preliminary inquiry was conducted on or about January 13, 1762. A report of it says the chief investigator "was sent for" to witness the strange goings-on at the Parsons house, so it's possible Parsons himself got things rolling. The investigator answering the call is identified only as "a gentleman" in the report. He first witnessed the alleged ghost answer several questions posed by Parsons in Elizabeth's bedroom. A cautious man, he then organized a team to better assess the case the next night. He was so cautious, in fact, that the group was comprised of a few more than *twenty* people.

They first examined the bed. Convinced there was nothing fishy there, they brought in Elizabeth. Through her, the spirit provided specifics of her murder. The poison had been administered in purl, otherwise known as wormwood ale. No one but Kent was involved in the murder. He would confess if "taken up" (presumably meaning arrested). He would be executed in three years (presumably known via ghostly prophecy). It was also learned that the spirit *could* and *would* manifest visually. Other questions were asked about the ghost's abilities. It could perceive members of the investigative team and even a timepiece belonging to one of them. The spirit claimed to be capable of leaving the house and of following Elizabeth if the girl were moved to some other house.[10] These last two answers became relevant to subsequent investigations.

Another team arrived on January 21 with the goal of debunking the case. One member entered Elizabeth's room alone and heard knocks that only repeated the ghost's previous answers and allegations. The others then joined him, and communication ceased. An investigator moved close to the girl's bed, and "a gentleman from the opposite side" (possibly Parsons) asked him to not sit so close.

"Sir, I came here to know the truth of the affair," asserted the ghost hunter, "and I think I have the right to place myself in any part of the room which is most suspicious."

The same investigator then asked if Elizabeth would be allowed to sleep at his house—with a room and a maid of her very own—but he was turned down by Parsons. That might have been a reasonable refusal. However, before the investigative team left, "the child appeared to be extraordinarily agitated." The scratching resumed, and the ghost was asked several questions about Lynes' family and about Kent. In many cases, "the ghost was unhappily mistaken."[11] Of course, this made the situation appear more like a ruse.

A more-thorough and better-remembered investigation was conducted on February 1. This one was led by the Reverend Stephen Aldrich, rector of St. John Clerkenwell Church. The church is where Lynes was interred in a burial vault, and concerns had been raised regarding the propriety surrounding that. A man identified as "Mr. Browne of Amen Corner" had publically wondered why Lynes had been laid to rest with no identifying plate affixed to her coffin and why yet another Lynes sister—one still living—had not been allowed to see the corpse before the coffin's lid was screwed into place. Browne also suggested that Kent's inheritance of Fanny Lynes' money was underhanded and she "was purely, and had sat up" the day before her death, implying her death was sudden. In contrast, "a worthy clergyman" who had been with Lynes during her final days contended that her death had been gradual and that medical experts "had pronounced her irrecoverable some days before her death."[12] I haven't found any evidence that the clergyman at Lynes' deathbed was Aldrich himself, but the rector of St. John's might have been acting to distance his church, if not Kent, from the taint of these ugly allegations.

Aldrich had a plan. We've seen that the ghost claiming to be Lynes said it could leave the premises and follow Elizabeth to other houses. With approval for a careful probe into the case from London's mayor, which gave more force to the plan, Aldrich met with Parsons "to ask him in respect of the time when his child should be brought to Clerkenwell." Parsons gave his consent—that is, under certain conditions. These conditions were refused because they would have undermined the examination. For example, the father suggested Elizabeth be accompanied by a woman he said was neutral and unconnected to the affair. Upon inquiry, however, this woman was rejected for being the opposite of neutral and unconnected. Eventually, Parsons succumbed, agreeing even to remain in the parlor while Elizabeth, attended by "a lady of character and fortune," was placed in a carefully arranged bed in a carefully arranged bedroom for examination by a group of qualified men.[13] This time, the communicative ghost would have to make itself known outside of the Cock Lane house and with no potential confederates in attendance.

Aldrich was prudent when assembling his paranormal team. Among them was John Douglas, another clergyman and the author of *The Criterion; or, Miracles Examined* (1754). That's the short title. Douglas's standpoint is made clear in the book's *full* title. It sharply contrasts the evidence for miracles mentioned in the New Testament, which are "TRUE," with evidence for miracles alleged to have occurred afterward, which "May Be FALSE."[14] Though Douglass went on to become a bishop in 1787, another team member is probably better remembered. Samuel Johnson stands among the greats of Britain's literary heritage. One of his outstanding contributions is *A Dictionary of the English Language* (1755), a nine-year project that produced a resource relied upon by countless speakers and writers for well over a century.

Johnson is credited with chronicling this decisive investigation for *Gentleman's Magazine*.[15] I'll now follow this document. It was "by the invitation of the Rev. Mr. Aldrich" that the team gathered "for the examination of the noises supposed to be made by a departed spirit, for the detection of some enormous crime." From about 10:00 p.m. to 11:00 p.m., the ghost hunters observed Elizabeth, who "had, with proper caution, been put to bed by several ladies" at Aldrich's residence. Nothing occurred, so they moved downstairs and "interrogated the father of the girl, who denied, in the strongest terms, any knowledge or belief in fraud." By this time, the nocturnal surveillance of Athenodorus had become routine ghost-hunting procedure. However, the witness interrogation in this case seems driven more by the debunking impulse of Deshoulières than Glanvill's careful gathering of firsthand data.

It wasn't Parsons who slipped up, though. It was the ghost—specifically, two instances of the ghost failing to communicate. First, after their interview with Parsons, the team was summoned by the women who were keeping tabs on Elizabeth upstairs. They had heard the scratching and knocking! The girl was awake and, sure enough, she had "felt the spirit like a mouse upon her back." One of the investigators told her to keep her arms in plain sight. With their test subject in this position, the ghost hunters bid the phantom to manifest itself in some way: "by appearance, by impression on the hand or body of anyone present, by scratches or knocks, or by any other agency." Nothing happened, though.

Second, the spirit was reminded of a promise it had made. Johnson explains:

> The supposed spirit had before publically promised, by an affirmative knock, that it would attend one of the gentlemen into the vault under the church of St. John, Clerkenwell, where the body is deposited, and give a token of her presence there by a knock upon her coffin.

It was time for this promissory note to be redeemed.

The team arrived at the church around 1:00 a.m. The person to whom the ghostly arrangements had been made went into the vault. No knocks were heard. Next, several people—William Kent among them—entered the vault. Still, nothing out of the ordinary was experienced.

The team returned to where Elizabeth was spending the night. They "examined the girl, but could draw no confession from her," says Johnson. Sometime between 2:00 and 3:00 that night, Elizabeth asked to be allowed to go home. No doubt, she was exhausted. Her request was granted, and she left with her father.

Based on what they experienced—namely, nothing —the esteemed ghost hunters had little choice when making their decision: the entire thing was a hoax. "It is therefore the opinion of the whole assembly," Johnson says, "that the child had some art of making or counterfeiting particular noise, and that there is no agency of any higher cause." [16] The term "art" here likely implies *artifice* rather than anything more complimentary. Despite the financial tensions between Parsons and Kent, the finger was pointed at Elizabeth.

In fact, examinations of the daughter continued. The next week, she was put to bed in a series of houses with results ranging from complete silence to "strong whispering" and "knockings and scratching exceedingly loud, which terrified the family, so that it was desired the child might be removed," according to *The London Magazine.* Meanwhile, William Kent was still obliged to defend his innocence. The same article says someone had speculated aloud that the ghost of Fanny Lynes failed to knock on her coffin that night because her body had been removed. The rumor gained enough sway that Kent, accompanied by other functionaries from St. John, went back to the vault. There, the

CERTAIN NOCTURNAL DISTURBANCES

undertaker identified the coffin, and it "was opened before Mr. K—, and a very awful shocking sight it was." In other words, the coffin was *not* empty, and to defend his innocence, Kent had been pushed to gaze at the decomposing remains of the woman he had loved. The report of this event was placed right before a lengthy quotation from the pamphlet *Mystery Revealed,* which is written from the viewpoint that Kent was being mistreated.[17] Whether or not Elizabeth was winning any sympathy among the many following the story, attitudes toward Kent seemed to be shifting in his favor.

At least, that was true of the jury who passed a judgment of *guilty* on both of Elizabeth's parents, along with a few others, for conspiring to injure Kent's character. The verdict came on July 10, 1762. But not everyone had turned against Parsons. Along with two years in prison, he was required to appear on a pillory. Rather than having rotten vegetables thrown at him as he stood hunched with his head and arms locked in place, the convicted man "was treated with great humanity, and several of the spectators gave him money."[18] In the end, one might wonder what Kent— and Elizabeth, too, once she was older—thought of this display of compassion.

A Third Victim Was One of the Ghost Hunters

Young Elizabeth Parsons asked if she could go home after being pressured to confess at 2:00 a.m. William Kent, facing accusations of concealing a murder, entered a crypt and watched as the coffin lid was raised from the mother of his unborn child. It's tough to review the Cock Lane Ghost case without being touched by its victims. Perhaps not as strikingly as these two, there was another victim involved, too. Samuel Johnson was branded a superstitious fool for

76

having bothered to investigate the reality of such a highly dubious ghost. The charge was misleading, but it lingered long after the great author's death.

Johnson's reputation for being easily duped by ghosts seems to start with Charles Churchill's satirical poem "The Ghost," the first half of which appeared in 1762. The work is so long that it wasn't published in full until the following year. A common interpretation of this narrative poem posits that the character Pomposo is a representation of Johnson. As pompous as his name implies, Pomposo is described as:

> . . . insolent and loud,
> Vain idol of a *scribbling* crowd,
> . . .
> Who, proudly seiz'd of Learning's throne,
> Now damns all Learning but his own;
> . . .
> Who, to increase his native strength,
> Draws words, six syllables in length
> With which, assisted with a frown,
> By way of Club, he knocks us down.[19]

"Club" is capitalized because it's a punning reference to an organization called The Club, which was made up of Johnson and other literary men. Other signs that Pomposo is a stand-in for Johnson are his being a hero among the literati (i.e., the "scribbling crowd"), an educated man, and a punctilious doyen of vocabulistics, meaning he knew a lot of fancy words.

This *might* still be drawn too broadly to bring Johnson to mind, though, so Churchill sharpens his point by having Pomposo join two others in search of a ghost named Fanny in a burial vault. The poet paints this trio of ghost hunters as open to the possibility of the Cock Lane ghost's authenticity, if not simply mystified by it. Pomposo and his associates are acting to determine *whether or not* Fanny is real:

If it be *True,* before we've done,
We'll make it glaring as the Sun;
If it be *false,* admit no doubt,
Ere Morning's dawn we'll find it out.[20]

This is probably a deliberate distortion created by Churchill. There are strong indications that Aldrich's team was intent on *debunking* the Cock Lane case, from their pressuring confessions of fakery from both Parsons and Elizabeth to the conclusion they drew from only one night's work.

Of course, Churchill's harsh treatment didn't persuade everyone. Johnson retained many, many admirers. In 1764, an anonymous critic addressed the issue by first explaining that Johnson had once judged Churchill's poetry as having "but little merit," an evaluation stated in confidence. The belittled man somehow learned about this, though, and "he resolved to requite this private opinion with a public one." His next poem was "The Ghost," and in it, "he has drawn this gentleman under the character of Pomposo; and those who disliked Johnson allowed it to have merit." Nonetheless, while the critic deems Churchill's talents to be noteworthy, he adds that they pale in comparison to Johnson's.[21] Regardless of how seriously readers took the poem, it is interesting that a man became a target for satire for having agreed to join a ghost hunt.

Then Churchill's seed took root. With time, Johnson became remembered as a great yet gullible man. A year after Johnson's death in 1784, a biography about him was published. The anonymous author praises the focal figure's intelligence and insight but contrasts these to his lack of *"practical* knowledge of mankind" and his inability "to resist, at all times, the infinite varieties of its impositions, as particularly appeared from his credulity in the celebrated affair of the Cock Lane Ghost, in 1762, and his acquiescence at least, if not belief, in the general doctrine of spirits." A couple of years later, John Hawkins' far more thorough biography—some 600 pages long!—says about the same thing regarding "the credit [Johnson] for some time gave to the idle story of the Cock Lane ghost." Toward the middle of the next century, Thomas Babbington Macaulay was still saying that Johnson "had been weak enough to pay serious attention to a story about a ghost which haunted a house in Cock Lane, and had actually gone himself . . . in the hope of receiving a communication from the perturbed spirit." Given this depiction of Johnson's relation to the case, it makes sense that the image spread to other forms of writing. In Herman Melville's 1851 novel *Moby Dick,* for instance, the narrator asks, "Are you a believer in ghosts, my friend? There are other ghosts than the Cock-Lane one, and far deeper men than Doctor Johnson who believe in them."[22] Smart, insightful, deep—but credulous when it came to ghosts—is how many came to view Johnson in the decades following the Cock Lane investigation.

This is odd, given that Aldrich's team *debunked* that haunting. James Boswell makes this very point in yet another biography of Johnson, this one published in 1791. Drawing from their many years of close friendship, Boswell turns to Johnson's stance on ghosts:

> He has been ignorantly misrepresented as weakly credulous upon that subject. . . . [H]e was willing to inquire into the truth of any relation of supernatural agency, a general belief of which has prevailed in all nations and ages. But so far was he from being the dupe of implicit faith, that he examined the matter with a jealous attention, and no man was more ready to refute its falsehood when he had discovered it.

Boswell then mentions "the absurd credulity imputed to Johnson" in Churchill's Pomposo caricature and reminds any reader still "under an impression that Johnson was thus foolishly deceived" by the Cock Lane case that, no, he "was one of those by whom the imposture was detected."[23] It's about as illogical as calling Deshoulières a sucker for the supernatural because she proved that a "ghost" was a dog.

Nevertheless, those wishing to perpetuate the image of Johnson as a believer in ghosts pointed to his writing. In his novel titled *The Prince of Abissinia: A Tale* (1759), we read: "There is no people, rude or learned, among whom apparitions of the dead are not related and believed. This opinion, which, perhaps, prevails as far as human nature is diffused, could become universal only by its truth." While it's true that Johnson *wrote* this, he did not exactly *say* it. This is a work of fiction, and that passage comes from the mouth of a character named Imlac. This distinction wasn't always respected. One critic declared that Johnson's "tendency to superstitious credence . . . is strongly evinced in" that passage, for example, and another claims it to be "the opinion of the judicious Johnson." Again, Boswell responds to this error, saying Imlac's words reveal the author's talent for expressing "the arguments of those who believe in the appearance of departed spirits, a doctrine which it is a mistake to suppose that he himself ever positively held."[24] Of course, there *are* such things as autobiographical characters in fiction, but there's always some portion of imagination in them, too. There's probably a trace of J.R.R. Tolkien in his imaginary characters—but he wasn't actually a hobbit himself.

Perhaps the best summary of Johnson's view of ghosts is found in a passage that is often quoted when that topic is raised. Again, it's found in Boswell's book:

> It is wonderful that five thousand years have now elapsed since the creation of the world, and still it is undecided whether or not there has ever been an instance of the spirit of any person appearing after death. All argument is against it; but all belief is for it.[25]

In the 1800s, the term "agnostic" was introduced to describe someone who refrains from believing or disbelieving in supernatural entities, especially God. Johnson, it appears, had an agnostic stance on ghosts. He had more than a passing interest in them, though, because ghosts seemed to stir in him a sense of *wonder*.

Pretty typical for a ghost hunter.

Roads Leading to—and Away from—Cock Lane

When the Cock Lane ghost announced its reason for returning—to ensure that a murderer be punished—it continued a tradition that had persisted for centuries. In an extensive chronology of the evolution of ghosts in Western Civilization, R.C. Finucane tracks spirits purported to return to the earthly plane "to name the guilty parties responsible for their deaths" as far back as Ovid's *Fasti*, published in the year 8 CE, and Apuleius's *Golden Ass*, published the following century.

One such case happened in 1690, about 70 years before Cock Lane, but it helps explain why Fanny Lynes' alleged return from the grave was treated with varying degrees of seriousness. Finucane explains that William Barick impregnated a woman named Mary, wed her, and then grew bored with her. As they were strolling along in what is now North Yorkshire, England, "William turned on this wife, battering her about the head then forcing her into a pond where he drowned her." He buried her nearby. A week passed. Mary's brother-in-law, Thomas, was working beside this pond and observed "what looked like a woman" dressed similarly to Mary. The figure disappeared into the air, though, and Thomas mentioned the weird vision to his wife. The woman "began to fear that her sister had been killed." They asked Barick about Mary—who was *missing*—and found his explanation flimsy enough that Thomas involved the mayor of York. After Barick was arrested, he confessed, and the body was discovered. Even so, the evidence that led to his conviction included "the mute apparition, which Thomas described in court." The story behind the Parsons haunting fit nicely with this long tradition of ghosts being unable to rest until their murderers were punished, giving the allegations enough weight for investigation. This also explains why some believers showed their support to Parsons as he was crouched in the pillory.

Furthermore, Lynes wasn't the first ghost to communicate via knocking. In 1528, Adrian Montalambert recorded a case involving a ghostly nun in Lyons, France, adding that he had been an eyewitness to the events. I follow Finucane's translation of that chronicle. A nun named Alis was ejected from a Lyons convent for "bad behavior." She grew ill in 1524 and prayed to the Virgin Mary for permission to be buried on the convent grounds. Two years later, Anthoinette, a nun still at the convent, was asleep when she "felt something lift her veil and kiss her." Anthoinette assumed it was just a dream—until "she began to hear light tapping sounds from the earth beneath her feet" a few days later. Montalambert interrupts the narrative to say he had heard these spectral raps frequently and discovered that the spirit would knock as many times as he requested. But, as with Elizabeth Parsons, Anthoinette had to be present to act as a medium for the ghost.

The news spread throughout Lyons. Meanwhile, Anthoinette theorized that the spirit belonged to the late Alis, who she had known and who had been appearing in her dreams. "The spirit, being conjured, affirmed that this was true," says Finucane (without clarifying exactly *how* the spirit was conjured. Perhaps it was simply called by name.) Through a rudimentary code, the abbess determined the burial wishes of Alis. Attempting to grant them, though, "a great disturbance arose and violent knockings bombarded the ears of the good nuns" as Alis's bones were brought into the church. An investigation was held by the Bishop of

Lyons with Montalambert at his side. After first expelling any evil spirits from the medium and the room—probably because of the ruckus that accompanied Alis's bones entering the church—the Bishop questioned the ghost. About forty exchanges were recorded, Alis answering with either yes, no, or silence. Finucane points out that "half the questions referred to purgatorial doctrines," the answers confirming Catholic beliefs then being challenged by advocates of Lutheranism.

In the end, the communicative ghost found forgiveness, was buried on convent grounds, and escaped Purgatory. As sort of a thank-you, Alis manifested before Anthoinette as "a nun of great stature, whose face was veiled" and then as "a weak voice," which confirmed her identity. Finally, "by means of a flurry of knocks, Alis announced her entry into paradise." Finucane says that "Montalambert concludes his account by once again referring to the false Lutheran heretics and their damnable sect." The publication was clearly part of a religious debate, this one involving Catholic versus Protestant views of Purgatory.[26] Nonetheless, the notion of spectral communication via knocking had preceded the Cock Lane incident by over 200 years.

Much closer to the Parsons' residence in terms of time and country was the witch, ghost, or poltergeist haunting the Mompesson family in 1662-63. As discussed in the previous chapter, Joseph Glanvill recorded a variety of manifestations in *Sadducismus Triumphatus,* but among them was the knocking that seemed to confirm the presence of Satan and of the beggar whose drum had been confiscated.[27] Unfortunately, no one there appears to have attempted anything more complex or even to have continued this method of communication to learn more.

The same is true of a poltergeist said to have paid a two-month visit to Epworth Rectory in Lincolnshire, England, in 1716. This was the residence of John Wesley, who went on to launch the Methodist movement. Recounting the case in

Historic Ghosts and Ghost Hunters (1908), H. Addington Bruce says that, amid diverse audible, visual, and tactile materializations, "if one stamped his foot, 'Old Jeffrey,' as the younger children named the ghost, would knock precisely as many times as there had been knockings." Bruce advises caution, though, because key documents of the case include those written from nine to 68 years *after* the haunting. Looking solely at the letters "written at the time of the disturbances" eliminates many of the wilder manifestations and turns the haunting into "a matter of knocks, groans, tinglings, squeaks, creakings, crashings, and footsteps."[28] Like the proverbial angler's estimate of the size of the netted fish, stories have a tendency to become enhanced and exaggerated with repeated telling.

While Mompesson's Drummer and Wesley's Old Jeffrey couldn't compete with Sister Alis in terms of communication, none of them gained the widespread notoriety for communication that the ghost of "Scratching Fanny" Lynes had. Indeed, the Cock Lane haunting was discussed and reinterpreted through the 1800s and afterward. In at least one important case, it also seems to have some shaping influence, however subtle.

As mentioned in the telltale bones discussion of Chapter One, in 1848, the Fox sisters of Rochester, New York, claimed to have made contact with the ghost of a murder victim. This was yet another knocking ghost, and it was quickly discovered that details could be gotten by asking questions tailored to a certain number of knocks. In this fashion, a man named John C. Bell came to be accused of the terrible crime. As had Kent all those years before him, Bell was forced to defend his innocence.[29] History was repeating itself, and within another complex mix of social factors came another burst of interest, controversy, and investigation.

In the wake of the news from Rochester, several writers pointed out the similarities between it—and, by extension, the growing number of mediums who used spirit "rapping" to converse with the dead—and the Cock Lane case. In 1853, for instance, an article titled "The Ghost of the Cock Lane Ghost" appeared in *Household Words,* a magazine edited by none other than Charles Dickens. (Dickens certainly enjoyed a good ghost story, but he was well known for being skeptical about Spiritualism.) After noting that Spiritualist exhibitions had crossed the Atlantic to Britain, the witty writer recounts the Cock Lane haunting through a series of questions and answers: "*Q.* Who was the first Medium? *A.* Little Miss Parsons. *Q.* Who was she? *A.* The daughter of the clerk at St. Sepulchre's. . . . " Switching, then, to a standard editorial format, the writer points out that, upon being "tested fairly by a perfect stranger," the Fox sisters "rapped out nothing but blunders." More incriminating evidence is then added.[30] Readers are left to conclude that Spiritualism, following in the tradition of Cock Lane, is a bunch of hooey.

Spiritualist sympathizers, on the other hand, reframed the haunting and aimed a spotlight on Elizabeth Parsons. The girl was an accomplished medium, according to William Howitt, author of a book with the almost-overwhelming title of *The History of the Supernatural in All Ages and Nations and in All Churches, Christian and Pagan, Demonstrating a Universal Faith* (1863). In an 1868 article in *The Spiritual Magazine,* Howitt focuses the lens of Spiritualism on several events that had been reported over the long history of *Gentleman's Magazine.* Once he reaches the coverage of the Cock Lane incident, Howitt points out that Parsons and Elizabeth "steadfastly denied any imposition." He explains the ghost's failure to make its presence known near Lynes' coffin to the fact that the Aldrich's investigation team "did not take the little girl with them, and not having the medium, they of course had no manifestation." In the end, "a careful examination of this story by modern lights, and the rules of regular evidence, have only tended to prove that the manifestations of the ghost were genuine enough."[31]

To fully appreciate Howitt's reinterpretation of the case, it can help to look at how those maintaining it was a hoax explained why such a grand deception was perpetrated. Was Parsons holding a grudge against Kent for suing him over the debt? For a long time, that was how history portrayed it. In *A New and Accurate History and Survey of London, Westminster, Southwark, and Places Adjacent,* published in 1766, the case is recorded as "a wicked contrivance to be revenged on Mr. K—t for suing for a trifle of money he had lent." A century later, in the popular magazine *All the Year Round,* Parsons is still pegged as the "impudent contriver" of the ruse because he "had a spite against a Norfolk gentleman who had once lodged with him, and afterwards sued him for a debt."[32] To say otherwise, as Howitt did, was fairly bold.

In the early 1900s, Bruce again boldly challenged this entrenched notion, but in a decidedly different way than Howitt had. In the Cock Lane chapter of *Historic Ghosts and Ghost Hunters,* Bruce declares it "preposterous to suppose that for so slight a cause as a dispute over twelve pounds Clerk Parsons and his associates would conspire to ruin a man's reputation and if possible take his life," and even more absurd to attempt such retaliation in the wild way they did. This is a point well worth considering, and other scholars have delved into how Parsons might have acted alongside Methodist-leaning clergy to promote a belief in ghostly intervention that was generally snubbed by the Anglican Church.[33] Unless a lot more communicative ghosts come forward with verifiable information, the reasons behind the hoax will probably have to remain dead and buried.

For now, we're stuck with speculation, and Bruce's counterargument to the theory involving Parsons' revenge is an eye-opening, if not jaw-dropping, one. Not one to waffle, he asserts, "The more likely, nay the only defensible solution of the problem, is" that those who suffered imprisonment— and Kent, too—were all "victims of the uncontrollable impulses of a hysterical child." In other words, pre-teen Elizabeth is the *culprit,* not the medium or one of the victims.

To defend this accusation, Bruce makes a number of very shaky assertions. A journalist with an interest in psychology, he was only 18 years younger than Sigmund Freud, and psychoanalysis was still in a fairly early stage of development. Therefore, we might forgive Bruce for dubbing Elizabeth Parsons to be "a striking and singular instance of 'dissociation.'" With no real evidence at all, he argues that Elizabeth was emotionally close to Frances Lynes and, "whether consciously or unconsciously," it was the daughter, not the father, who held the grudge against Kent. Upon learning of Lynes' death, Elizabeth snapped, blaming Kent for the death and seeing him as a murderer. In an effort to ensure justice, "the neurotic child [developed] a full-fledged second personality," according to Bruce. In the end, the shock of her parents' arrest evoked "at least partial reintegration" and the end of "the secondary self, the much debated, malevolent Cock Lane ghost."[34] I strongly suspect that psychoanalysts even in 1908 would have cringed at this ungrounded diagnosis from an amateur.

Of greater interest—at least, in terms of ghost hunting—is the remarkable fact that an alleged haunting from 1762 was still a source of interest, investigation, theorization, and debate in the 1900s. People were still striving to solve the mystery of Cock Lane.

The Paranormal Investigation Team Is Not New

Many people in the early 2000s have a rough image of a paranormal investigation team. Four or five members. Often—but certainly not always—in their 20s or 30s. Dark clothes and a good supply of electronic gadgetry. Sometimes very serious expressions in their promotional photos. Frequently, a name that doubles as a catchy acronym—for example, Advanced Ghost Hunters of Seattle-Tacoma has a great one: AGHOST. One might wonder how this image contrasts with or compares to the team of paranormal investigators that Aldrich assembled from, as Johnson put it, "many gentlemen, eminent for their rank and character."[35] (Would it help if we called them Cock Lane's Eminent and Noted Spook Examiners, a.k.a. CLEANSE?)

Just as Lynes' ghost wasn't the first alleged to communicate via knocking, Aldrich's team wasn't the first of its kind. Finucane relates an investigation held by an earlier group. In 1534, the Franciscan monks in Orleans, France, went public with their encounter with a ghost. In one early chronicle, the ghost spoke, but records of about two centuries later say it communicated by knocking. A reversal of the once-wayward, now-penitent nun Alis, this remorseful ghost found herself longing to be *expelled* from a Catholic cemetery because, in life, she had made the terrible mistake of converting to Lutheranism. Or was this just an anti-Protestant fable the monks had invented? The case reached the King's ear, and Finucane says, "Francis I appointed a mixed clerical-lay commission to examine the case." Some of the monks "tried to slip out of town," so a group of them were detained in holding cells. After a few weeks, "the friars involved withdrew their earlier claims, now admitting that they had never actually encountered a spirit of any kind." The instigators were condemned to "be burnt alive" as an example to others, but "royal grace commuted the sentences to banishment."[36] Comparing this to Aldrich's team, it seems as if these ghost committees tended to *debunk*.

However, some *affirmed* ghostly observations. In late 1642, Charles I, King of England, Scotland, and Ireland, sent a party of men on a very curious task. According to a pamphlet of the period, "Colonel Lewis Kirke, Captain Dudley, Captain Wainman, and three other gentlemen of credit" were delegated to evaluate reports of supernatural activity in what is now called Kineton, Warwickshire. Specifically, the haunted site was Edgehill, where one of the very first battles in the English Civil War had occurred in October. Spectral reenactments of the battle had been observed that Christmas Eve, Christmas Night, and weekends thereafter. The pamphlet says that "strange and portentous apparitions of two jarring and contrary armies" had manifested "where the corporeal armies had shed so much blood." The phenomena started at midnight and lasted an hour. It included the sounds of the drums, musket fire, and horses neighing along with the sights of the soldiers clashing and the military colors of the King in contrast to those of Parliament. The first witnesses were shepherds, travelers, and others whose word might not have carried much weight, but once a local Justice of the Peace and a minister both saw and heard the same military echoes, something had to be done.

But what *could* be done? After interviewing witnesses, the investigators performed nocturnal surveillance— "wherein they heard and saw the aforementioned prodigies." The military officers later swore to their King that they even recognized some of the ghosts as having been those slain in action. The pamphleteer ends the account by proclaiming that the haunting is a sign of God's anger over the civil war, "which He, in His good time will finish, sending a sudden peace between His Majesty and Parliament."[37] Evoking the fear and awe of God is an effective way to persuade, and it's not unreasonable to assume the pamphlet was written less as authentic history and more as a way to promote peace.

Moving about twenty years forward, another royally appointed team of ghost hunters went back to debunking mode when they visited the Mompesson haunting. Glanvill refers to "the gentlemen the King sent," saying that, when they conducted nocturnal surveillance there, "the house was quiet, and nothing was seen nor heard that night, which was confidently and with triumph urged by many to be a confutation of the story." Glanvill then points out the poor logic of basing such a conclusion on a *single* night's investigation, especially given the many other reports of strange activity. He explains:

> This is a common argument of those that deny the existence of apparitions: they have travelled all hours of the night, and never saw anything worse than themselves (which may well be) and thence they conclude that all pretended apparitions are fancies or impostures.[38]

Glanvill uses the adjective "pretended" here to mean *professed* or *claimed*. (The idea that something pretended is *feigned* or *playfully imagined* rose in the 1800s.) He makes a valid point, one that could apply to the conclusion drawn by Aldrich's team after only one night. Of course, the court trial that convicted Parsons and his collaborators hopefully relied on a good deal more evidence than that group's findings.

The Aldrich team was far from the last of the "ghost committees." In 1833, a parsonage in Fakenham, England, was the site of another knocking ghost. This one did more than knock, though, and wasn't as easily explained. The Reverend Mr. Steward and his family weren't able to discover the cause of the phenomena, and according to a newspaper report, the knocking became "more violent, until it had now arrived at such a frightful pitch that one of the servants has left through absolute terror." The noises started at 2:00 a.m. and continued until sunrise, moving from place to place. Moans were heard, too, sounding like "a soldier being whipped," accompanied by rattling and crashes. Intrigued neighbors, along with each family member, claimed to have witnessed the spectral display.

At some point, Steward assembled a team comprised of four clergymen, one of their wives, and one surgeon. On the night of their investigation, "the noises were even louder and of longer continuance than usual," as if the entity were aware of their presence. "The disturber was conjured to speak," says the article, "but answered only by a low hollow moaning, but on being requested to give three knocks, it gave three most tremendous blows, apparently in the wall." The committee departed in confusion, and the newspaper reporter closes by expressing a hunch that a hoax would eventually be unveiled. Despite that prediction, the reporter says that, given

> the respectability and superior intelligence of the parties who have attempted to investigate the secret, we are quite willing to allow to the believers of earthly visitations of ghosts all the support which this circumstance will afford to their creed—that of unaccountable mystery.[39]

The one-night investigation and, to an extent, the spectral phenomena itself are similar to the Cock Lane case. However, the committee's conclusion—or lack thereof—is very different.

This kind of short-term ghost committee went on to be formed for at least another fifty years—and thousands of miles away from Cock Lane. In 1874, a trio of eminent gentlemen from Oakland, California, met to investigate a haunted house. Following the centuries-old pattern, the team was comprised of both clergy and lay people: a lawyer named William W. Crane, Jr., a Congregationalist pastor named John Knox McLean, and a professor of geology and natural history at UC-Berkeley named Joseph Le Conte. Thomas B. Clarke was the owner of the alleged haunted house. According to one newspaper, the Clarke residence had been prey to inexplicable loud noises, moving furniture, and "a shrill shriek of mingled pain and rage." The manifestations lasted only three days, though, during which the Clarkes remained in the house. The ghost hunters couldn't comfortably take occupancy, and even nocturnal surveillance made little sense.

Undaunted, the trio approached their work and their final assessment with seriousness. Their thoroughness is apparent in a letter Clarke wrote to Crane, McLean, and Le Conte after their investigation: "My residence, my family, and my friends attended upon you for seven nights into unseasonable hours." The trio's work led to a restrained, carefully worded conclusion:

> [A]fter a careful examination of the construction of the house, and location of the furniture with respect to the persons present, after a patient hearing of witnesses, and, as we believe, an impartial weighing and comparison of the testimony, we find the evidence insufficient to indicate the action or presence of any supernatural, or of any occult natural agency whatever.[40]

Unlike the conclusion reached by Aldrich's team, which points a finger at Elizabeth's "art of making or counterfeiting particular noise," Crane, McLean, and Le Conte offer no *natural* explanation. Neither do they exactly say that what happened at Clarke's house *wasn't* supernatural or occult. They merely say they didn't find enough solid and reliable evidence to support the claim that there *was* something supernatural or occult occurring.

Meanwhile, the Victorians were putting a very new spin on the paranormal investigation team. Instead of a sort of impromptu assembly of investigators "eminent for their rank and character" in Johnson's terms, a number of Cambridge students began to meet to study ghosts and related topics. It's been remembered by various names: The Cambridge Association for Spiritual Inquiry, the Ghost Club, and the Ghostly Guild. Some of the members did well for themselves. Brooke Foss Westcott, who appears to be the one who founded the group, went on to become the Bishop of Durham. Edward White Benson became the Bishop of Truro and, afterward, the Archbishop of Canterbury. Sir Arthur Gordon went into politics, and Henry Bradshaw became a librarian.[41] Here, we see the spark that ignited two paranormal organizations that still exist, namely, the Ghost Club, founded in 1862, and the Society for Psychical Research, founded in 1882.

These long-lived organizations count on *teamwork* when it comes to nosing around locations said to be haunted. For instance, in its early years, the Society formed committees to focus on particular phenomena, such as thought-transference or mesmerism. One was called the Committee on Haunted Houses, and it recognized the challenges of short-term investigations. In one report, the committee spokesperson says that "fixed times for ghostly appearances could very rarely be determined; in most cases, if the investigation was to be carried on with any hope of success, the house must be continuously inhabited." In the next month's report, the Committee announced that it had found such an opportunity! There was "a small house near Hyde Park," where unexplained footsteps and an apparition had been witnessed. The resident/informant was deemed reliable—and he was moving out—so committee members "decided to take the house for a short time." Occupancy was shared by committee and other Society members, but no one was able "to record evidence of abnormal phenomena." Ending on a bright note, the reporter adds that the Committee "gained some experience in a rather difficult art, the negotiation for leases for 'haunted houses.'" How long this house was rented isn't stated, but a later Society investigation following the same model lasted over a year.[42] This form of group ghost hunting certainly didn't guarantee results, but it was an improvement on the single-night visits used with the Mompessons and the Parsons.

The 1874 Oakland haunting illustrates how the "ghost-hunter committee" model used in the 1642 Cock Lane and earlier cases had far-reaching, long-lasting application. If the work of such investigation teams was too brief to lead to worthwhile conclusions, this flaw was being addressed by the "haunted-house occupancy" model used by the Society. As shown in upcoming chapters, there *were* still ghost hunters flying solo. However, the many paranormal investigation teams in the 21st century can smile proudly, knowing their roots stretch back for centuries.

---

[1] Andrew Lang, *Cock Lane and Common-sense* (Longmans, Green, and Co., 1894) p. 161.

[2] For instance, H. Addington Bruce changes Kent's name to Knight and contradicts earlier accounts by saying Frances Lynes—whose ghost plays a key role in subsequent events—arrived *after* her sister's death rather than to care for her when she was sick. See *Historic Ghosts and Ghost Hunters* (Moffat, Yard, and Co., 1908) pp. 82, 86. News articles about the trial confirm the name William Kent. See, for example, *British Magazine* 3 (July 1762) p. 390.

[3] The table can be found on an unnumbered page toward the end of *The Book of Common Prayer, and Administration of the Sacraments and Other Rites and Ceremonies of the Church, According to the Use of the Church of England* (Printed by Thomas Baskett, 1749). One key document contends the couple *could* have married "had there been no issue born alive from his former wife," and the author says Kent wondered "why so small an obstacle as the birth of a child, that so short a time survived his mother, should prevent his happiness." This source is an anonymous pamphlet titled *The Mystery Revealed; Containing a Series of Transactions and Authentic Testimonials Respecting the Supposed Cock Lane Ghost* (printed for W. Bristow, 1762) pp. 5-6. The hard-to-find pamphlet was subsequently attributed to Oliver Goldsmith and reprinted in such books as *The Works of Oliver Goldsmith*, vol. 4 (John Murray, 1854) pp. 361-375.

[4] The pregnancy is noted in *Universal Magazine* 30 (January 1762) p. 45, and in *Mystery Revealed*, p. 10.

[5] Lynes' date of death is found in *Gentleman's Magazine* 32 (January 1762) p. 43.

[6] *London Magazine,* 31 (January 1762) p. 51.

[7] *Gentleman's Magazine,* p. 43; *Universal Magazine,* p. 45. The latter includes the report of Parsons having the walls checked and moving Elizabeth to a new room.

[8] Elizabeth Parson's naming Elizabeth Kent as the first ghost was reported in *Gentleman's Magazine,* p. 43. Regarding Elizabeth Kent's sluggish spirit, *Mystery Revealed* says the Kents wed in 1756. However, their marital bliss only lasted "about eleven months" due to the wife's death (p.4). This means she very likely died in 1757. The first visitation at Cock Lane would be in 1759 or 1760, two or three years later.

[9] Horace Walpole, "Letter CLXV," *Letters from the Honorable Horace Walpole to George Montagu, Esq., from the Year 1736 to the Year 1770* (Printed for Rodwell and Martin, 1818) pp. 277-278.

[10] *Gentleman's Magazine,* pp. 43-44.

[11] *Oxford Journal,* January 23, 1762, p. 3.

[12] *Gentleman's Magazine,* p. 43. There is also a discrediting of these allegations in *Mystery Revealed,* p. 14. Browne's accusations were publicized in an article titled "An Authentic Narrative of Several Particulars Relating to the Death of Miss Frances Lynes, Whose Ghost Is Supposed to Have Haunted an House in Cock Lane, West Smithfield," published in *The Royal Chronicle.* This information is in a report on the court case *The King v. Robert Browne* found in *A Digest of the Law Concerning Libels* (Printed by William Hallhead, 1778) p. 84.

[13] *London Magazine,* p. 51.

[14] John Douglas, *The Criterion; Or, Miracles Examined with a View to Expose the Pretensions of Pagans and Papists; to Compare the Miraculous Powers Recorded in the New Testament, with Those Said to Subsist in Later Times; and to Shew the Great and Material Difference Between Them in Point of the Evidence: From Whence It Will Appear that the Former are TRUE and the Latter May Be FALSE* (Printed for A. Millar, 1754) title page.

[15] That Johnson penned the anonymous article is stated by James Boswell, his knowledge having come from Douglas, in *The Life of Samuel Johnson, L.L.D.,* vol. 1 (Printed by Henry Baldwin, 1791) p. 220.

[16] *Gentleman's Magazine* 32 (February 1762) p. 81.

[17] *London Magazine* 31 (March 1762) pp. 150-151.

[18] The verdict is reported in *Gentleman's Magazine* 32 (July 1762) p. 339. The compassion shown to Parsons as he stood on the pillory is reported in *London Chronicle,* March 29-31, 1763, p. 310.

[19] Churchill's poem is comprised of four "books." The first two were published independently with the oddly tautological phrase "By the Author" under the title: *The Ghost* (Printed for the Author, and Sold by William Flexney, 1762). It was then released in full with "C. Churchill" identified as author: *The Ghost* (Printed for the Author, and Sold by William Flexney, 1763). The quotation is from pp. 55-56 of the latter source.

[20] Churchill, 1763, p. 53.

[21] "Memoirs of Mr. Charles Churchill," *The Scots Magazine* 26 (December 1764) p. 651.

[22] *The Life of Samuel Johnson, LL.D.* (Printed for R. Moncrieffe, et al., 1785) pp. 149-150. John Hawkins, "The Life of Dr. Samuel Johnson," *The Works of Samuel Johnson, LL.D.,* vol. 1 (Printed for J. Buckland, et al., 1787) pp. 436. Thomas Babbington Macaulay, "Samuel Johnson," *Harper's New Monthly* 14 (March 1857) pp. 491-492. Herman Melville, *Moby Dick* (Harper Brothers, 1851) p. 345.

[23] Boswell, vol. 1, p. 220.

[24] Samuel Johnson, *The Prince of Abissina: A Tale,* vol. 2 (Printed for R. and J. Dodsley, 1760) p. 41. It was then retitled *The History of Rasselas, Prince of Abissinia.* Examples of critics ascribing Imlac's comment to the author himself are found in "Reflections upon a Ghost Story of Lord Clarendon's," *The Christian Reformer* 5 (July 1819) p. 296, and J. Dennis, *Subversion of Materialism by Credible Attestation of Supernatual Occurences* (Upham, Collins, and Binns, 1826) p. 101. Boswell's counterargument to this is in *Life,* vol. 1, p. 186.

[25] Boswell, vol. 2, p. 190.

[26] R.C. Finucane, *Ghosts: Appearances of the Dead & Cultural Transformation* (Prometius, 1996) pp. 22, 126, 106-108. Finucane's source for the chronicle of Anis is Nicolas Lenglet-Dufresnoy's *Recueil de Dissertations Anciennes et Nouvelles: sur les Apparitions, les Visions & les Songes* (Chez Jean-Noël Leloup, 1751). See also Lang, pp. 110-113.

[27] Joseph Glanvill, *Sadducismus Triumphatus* (Printed for A.L., 1700) pp. 52-53 of the "Evidence" section.

[28] Bruce, pp. 43-44, 50.

[29] See Robert Dale Owen's *Footfalls on the Boundary of Another World* (J.B. Lippincott, 1859) pp. 291, 297.

[30] "Ghost of the Cock Lane Ghost," *Household Words* 6 (1852) pp. 317-19. This was not the only—or the first—example of attempting to debunk Spiritualism by comparing it to the Cock Lane fraud. The same strategy is used in 1851 by an anonymous author, who contends that the sounds around Elizabeth's bed "were produced by the girl, acting through the muscles, upon moving parts as in the case of the Rochester knockings. It might be suspected, even, that the Rochester rappers obtained a hint of their operations from the Cock-lane ghost." This comes from a pamphlet titled *Rochester Knockings! Discovery and Explanation of the Source of the Phenomena Generally Known as the Rochester Knockings* (George H. Derby, 1851) p. 57.

[31] William Howitt, "Evidences of Spiritualism in Modern Works of History and Literature," *Spiritual Magazine* 3 (May 1868) p. 202.

[32] John Entick, *A New and Accurate History and Survey of London, Westminster, Southwark, and Places Adjacent,* vol. 3 (Printed for Edward and Charles Dilley, 1766) p. 205. "Chronicles of London Streets: Charing Cross," *All the Year Round* 7 (March 2, 1872) p. 329.

[33] Bruce, pp. 98-99. Regarding the influence of clergy who sympathized with Methodism, specifically Reverends John Moore and Thomas Broughton, see Sasha Handley, *Visions of an Unseen World: Ghost Beliefs and Ghost Stories in Eighteenth-Century England* (Routledge, 2016) pp. 143-144.

[34] Bruce, pp. 99-101. Bruce's interest in psychology is evident in his having written *The Riddle of the Personality* (Moffat, Yard, and Co., 1908) and *Pyschology and Parenthood* (Dodd, Mead, and Co., 1915).

[35] *Gentleman's Magazine,* p. 81.

[36] Finucane, pp. 109-110. See also Lang, pp. 115-117.

[37] The original pamphlet is *A Great Wonder in Heaven, Shewing the Late Apparitions and Prodigious Noises of War and Battles Seen at Edge-hill, near Keinton in Northamptonshire...* (Printed for Thomas Jackson, 1642). It is reprinted in Lord Nugent's *Some Memorials of John Hampden, His Party, and His Times,* vol. 2 (John Murray, 1832) pp. 462-467. Nugent's reprint of the very rare pamphlet has served as a source for John H. Ingram's *The Haunted Homes and Family Traditions of Great Britain* (W.H. Allen, 1884) pp. 65-69, and W.W.H.'s "The Battle of Edge Hill and Its Ghost Story," *Argosy* 59 (1895) pp. 381-384.

[38] Glanvill, pp. 61-62 of the "Evidence" section.

[39] "A Real Ghost," *Glamorgan Monmouth and Brecon Gazette and Merthyr Guardian,* June 8, 1833, p. 2. The article is attributed to the *Norfolk Chronicle.*

[40] The manifestations are reported in "The Periodical Ghost. He Is Making Things Lively in Clarke's House in Oakland," *Daily Alta California,* April 27, 1874, p. 1. That the phenomena lasted only three days is found in James H. Hysop's "A Case of Poltergeist," *Proceedings for the American Society for Psychical Research* 7 (1913) pp. 233-251. The letters passed between Clarke and Crane, McLean, and Le Conte are reprinted in "Coming to a Focus. Pertinent Correspondence Between Mr. Clarke and the Ghost Committee," *Daily Alta California,* July 4, 1874, p. 1. For the trio's conclusion, see Hysop, p 251.

[41] Epes Sargent refers to the "Cambridge Association for Spiritual Inquiry, familiarly called the Ghost Club," in *Planchette; or, The Despair of Science* (Roberts Brothers, 1869) p. 203. G.W. Prothero calls it "The Ghostly Guild" in his biography *A Memoir of Henry Bradshaw, Fellow of King's College, Cambridge, and University Librarian* (Kegan Paul, Trench, and Co., 1888) p. 26, the same spot where he confirms Bradshaw's membership. Westcott's and Gordon's membership is confirmed in Arthur Westcott's *Life and Letters of Brooke Foss Westcott,* vol. 1 (Macmillan, 1903) p. 117; and Benson's is in Arthur Christopher Benson's *The Life of Edward White Benson,* vol. 1 (Macmillan, 1899) p. 98.

[42] "General Meeting," *Journal of the Society for Psychical Research* 1.3 (April 1884) p. 37. "Notices of Work Done by Committees," *Journal of the Society for Psychical Research* 1.4 (May 1884) pp. 51-52. The thirteen-month investigation is discussed by Frank Podmore in "Phantasms of the Dead from Another Point of View," *Proceedings of the Society for Psychical Research* 6 (November 29, 1889) pp. 255-270, 309-313.

CHAPTER FIVE

Purposeless Ghosts:
Jervis, Bolton, and Luttrell
at Hinton Ampner

Less than a decade after mobs had gathered to glimpse a ghost on Cock Lane, John Jervis (later known as the Earl of St. Vincent), John Bolton, and James Luttrell conducted a ghost hunt at a manor house called Hinton Ampner in Hampshire, England. Strange things had been occurring at the house ever since the Ricketts moved there in early 1765. There had been a variety of manifestations, mostly heard but also a few sightings of phantom figures. The ghost hunt took place in 1771. It was a bit of a disappointment. While the ghost hunters heard some of the weird noises, they were in no position at all to finish the ghosts' unfinished business or to exorcize the house. Instead, they advised the Ricketts to leave the mansion, and the family did so. The structure was pulled down about twenty years later.

The best evidence for this case comes from a chronicle written by Mary Ricketts for her children, who would have been too young to remember the haunting very well. The chronicle—describing the events as they happened from 1765 to 1771—wasn't made public until 1872, when it appeared as "A Hampshire Ghost Story" in the *Gentleman's Magazine.*[1] For convenience, I'll refer to this as the M.R. chronicle in honor of its primary author.

That is—its *alleged* primary author. There is little information given to explain why the document was published close to a century after its creation other than it had been mentioned in a memoir released two years earlier. Who brought it to *Gentleman's,* how this person acquired it, and whether or not permission to publish it had been gotten (or was needed) are all mysteries. Indeed, one might raise an eyebrow when comparing the M.R. chronicle to Robert Stephen Hawker's dubious claim of five years earlier, the one about his having located Parson Ruddle's diurnal (as discussed in Chapter Two). How reliable *is* the M.R. chronicle?

Well, there are interesting references to the Hinton Ampner haunting and to Ricketts keeping a journal that corroborate what was printed in *Gentleman's.* One of the earliest of these is in Sir Walter Scott's *Letters on Demonology and Witchcraft,* first released in 1830. The famous author discusses "accredited ghost stories usually told at the fireside," attributing their so-called credibility to "the general wish to believe" rather than to any solid evidence. The Hinton Ampner haunting is his example. "This is told as a real story," Scott scoffs, then asking, "who has heard or seen an authentic account" from either of the two ghost hunters or from the haunted woman.[2] In this regard, the M.R. chronicle certainly does feel as if it's been invented to meet Scott's challenge.

However, another reference is found in *Reminiscences for My Children,* an 1836 memoir written by Catherine Mary Howard. The haunting, investigation, and suggestion that it was a hoax are all covered in a single paragraph—albeit, a three-page paragraph. The haunting is given more attention by Frances Williams-Wynn in the 1864 memoir *Diaries of a Lady of Quality.* She says the source of information was a Mrs. Hughes, who—while eavesdropping "in her infancy"—heard the story narrated by a witness named Mrs. Gwyn. Despite this questionable reliability, there is mention of Ricketts keeping "a regular journal of the transactions of each night." The same Mrs. Hughes is relied on in *The Life and Letters of the Rev. Richard Harris Barham,* edited by his son and first printed in 1870. (This is the biography that sparked publication of the M.R. chronicle in *Gentleman's.*) Along with making some minor corrections to Hughes' secondhand story, Barham says it was "confirmed by many others," some of whom examined that journal.[3] If nothing else, it appears Ricketts *did* keep a detailed record of the ghostly goings-on at her house.

In addition, if the M.R. chronicle is not Mary Ricketts' actual record, it's certainly a clever fake. Rather than adding touches to make the tale more like a "tidy" ghost story found in fiction, as Hawker did with his alleged diurnal, this document adds the messy details one expects from an *actual* haunting. These include curious aberrations, such as "sounds of harmony" amid otherwise anguished or harsh vocalizations; easily misinterpreted physical phenomena such as knocking; and puzzles such as *two* phantom figures seen but *three* disembodied voices heard. There are also supplementary documents—letters and attestations—supporting the chronicle's authenticity. These bear the names of very real, very prominent, and very powerful persons, exposing a hoaxer to serious repercussions. Then again, those names belong to people who were dead by 1872: Rev. John Sargent, who died in 1833; John Jervis, 1823; Edward Jervis Ricketts, 1859; Osbourne Markham, 1827; and Martha H.G. Jervis, 1865. For every clue of authenticity, there seems to be another one suggesting a ruse.

Still, if someone held a poltergeist to my head and forced me to choose, I'd say the M.R. chronicle is authentic. I find it convincing enough to use it as the basis of the following timeline/retelling of the Hinton Ampner haunting.

1755: Henry Bilson Legge took ownership of Hinton Ampner. He "usually came there for one month every year during shooting season."[4]

1764: Legge died in April, and in December, the Ricketts began renting the mansion from his widow.

1765: In January, the family had settled in, but Mary Ricketts recalls that she "frequently heard noises in the night, as of people shutting or rather slapping doors with vehemence." Her husband, William Ricketts, looked into the sounds, but he found no explanation. Changing the locks had no effect.

About six months later, the eldest son's nurse clearly observed "a gentleman in a drab-coloured suit go into the yellow room." This was not a cause of concern—until she learned from a housemaid that there shouldn't have been a man there. To their bewilderment, they found no evidence that there had been a man at all.

That autumn, the groom saw a man dressed the same way. He also became unnerved upon finding there was no such man.

1767: Four persons in the kitchen "heard a woman come down the stairs, . . . whose clothes rustled as of the stiffest silk." They then saw a "female figure" quickly exit. "Their view of her was imperfect; but they plainly distinguished a tall figure in dark-coloured clothes." When they asked a man just then entering who it had been, he said he hadn't seen anyone.

1769: Despite continuing reports of strange noises, Mr. Ricketts left to attend to business in Jamaica. His wife was left with three small children and eight servants.

From her bedroom, Ricketts heard silk rustling and footsteps. Investigation granted no answers, and locking doors proved useless.

Summer, 1770: Lying in the yellow bedchamber— where the phantom in the drab suit had appeared five years earlier—Ricketts "plainly heard the footsteps of a man, with plodding step, walking towards the foot of my bed." She made a search, "but all in vain."

November 1770 to early 1771: Though the manifestation in the yellow room had alarmed Ricketts, she courageously remained there until the cold weather prompted her to move into the warmer "chintz bedroom." There, she occasionally heard "sounds of harmony" and, one night, "three distinct and violent knocks as given with a club." In the months following, she heard "a hollow murmuring that seemed to possess the whole house." Whether the night was calm or windy made no difference—the sound appeared either way.

February 1771: Elizabeth Godin, a servant, reported having heard "the most dismal groans and fluttering around her bed most part of the night."

April 1771: Still sleeping in the chintz room, Ricketts heard footsteps in the adjoining lobby. She listened at the door, and the steps seemed to approach her. Even with a couple of servants assisting, she was unable to discover the cause.

Midsummer 1771: Ricketts says that "the noises became every night more intolerable. They began before I went to bed and, with intermissions, were heard till after broad day in the morning. I could frequently distinguish articulate sounds, and usually a shrill female voice would begin, and then two others with deeper manlike tone seemed to join in the discourse." Though the voices were close to her, Ricketts could never make out specific words. Godin shared this experience.

August 1771: Given all that was occurring, the exhausted Ricketts contacted her brother, Captain Jervis. He arrived and went to work, seeking a solution and enlisting the assistance of Bolton, his servant, and Lutrell, a neighbor and fellow naval officer.

On the evening of the ghost hunt, Jervis and Bolton first gave the house a thorough examination, looking for possible hiding places and checking locked doors. Next, Jervis retired—remaining on "standby" and leaving Luttrell and Bolton to maintain surveillance from the chintz room. They were armed in case the threat proved to be less supernatural and more criminal. The next morning, at breakfast, Luttrell gave a report. He had heard footsteps in the lobby and called "Who goes there?" A presence "flitted past him," and he heard Jervis shout "Look against my door!" Indeed, the concerned brother was awake and had heard something approach. Now, Luttrell and Jervis were both up and alert, and both "heard various other noises, examined everywhere, [and] found the staircase door fast secured" as it had been. Jervis and Bolton confirmed that the servants were all in their rooms. Jervis and Lutrell had remained on watch until dawn.

When Ricketts asked about a door slam she had heard, Lutrell assured her it had *not* been caused by any of the investigators. Jervis also admitted to hearing "dreadful groans and various noises" when he was in his bedroom.

It was Lutrell who first declared that "the house was an unfit residence for any human being." Jervis quietly agreed. The brother then sat up every night of the week he remained at Hinton Ampner. One of these nights, Ricketts heard a gunshot followed by groans near her room. Jervis also heard it, but a nurse (presumably not far away) had not. This phenomena of a loud noise being heard by some—but not others nearby—was repeated several times. Again, Jervis advised his sister to take her children and herself somewhere else.

She did so before the end of that month.

September 1771: A Mr. Sainsbury, agent for Lady Hillsborough, wrote to inform Ricketts that he and two others were intending to perform another night's stakeout at the house. Robert Camis, a servant who assumed caretaker duties after the Ricketts left, sent another letter to update Sainsbury's follow-up investigation. Sainsbury interviewed Camis's mother about what had been experienced there. The son adds that Sainsbury offered a reward of fifty guineas for information leading to the conviction of anyone committing a hoax.

November 1771: Camis wrote to Ricketts to say that his mother and sister had heard "a dismal groaning very loud" while at Hinton Ampner.

After that, little is known. The M.R. chronicle ends with a document titled "Narrative by Martha H.G. Jervis," dated July 10, 1818. The writer, presumably Captain Jervis's daughter, says she "called on old Lucy Camis," presumably Robert's mother, and got additional substantiation of the manifestations at Hinton Ampner. This ends with a quick mention of a Mr. Lawrence, who "afterwards took possession of the house." The aged woman contends that "a female figure" was seen by a housemaid, "but of the truth of this she could not vouch."[5] Still, if we can trust that Robert's mother and sister heard that groan after the Ricketts had departed, the hoaxer theory loses some weight. Apparently, no such hoaxer had ever been caught despite Sainsbury's reward.

There are a few slight discrepancies between the M.R. chronicle and the references to it found in the memoirs. For instance, both Williams-Wynn and Barham imply that William Ricketts' sailed for Jamaica very soon after he had rented Hinton Ampner.[6] Of course, they're paraphrasing the same woman who, many years earlier, secretly heard the story. Nonetheless, we are now in a good position to see what this haunting can teach us about ghosts and ghost hunting in the decades and centuries that followed.

Rickety Theories

The earliest theory widely published is that the whole haunting was a deception of some kind or another. As mentioned above, in 1830, Scott said the story of the haunting and ghost hunt were products of a desire to believe, not of actual evidence. Even if eyewitness testimony were found, he says, one must ask if it "might not be in some degree tinged" by superstition. Jervis, after all, was a seaman, and that bunch has a "tendency to superstition."[7] A problem here is that Jervis was far from the only witness. According to the other documents, there were *many*— residents of the house along with visitors—who experienced the phenomena, especially in regard to the strange noises.

Instead of self-deception, then, perhaps these people were the victims of foul play. Howard suggests this by declaring that

> an old gardener who had long been attached to the house confessed, on his dying bed, that preferring to be the sole master there, and finding that a widow and her daughter would not spend much money, or add to his profits, he had contrived, in concert with the lady's maid whom he married, to make those alarming noises by the help of a subterraneous passage that connected the garden with the house.

Not only does Howard admit that this is based on hearsay,[8] there are problems with facts and logic. Mrs. Ricketts *wasn't* a widow and she had *more than one* child. How a gardener would benefit financially by being "the sole master there" isn't explained. If the widow and daughter were cheapskates, wouldn't it make more sense to strive toward getting them replaced with tenants more generous? In addition, while deathbed confessions probably *have* been made from time to time in real life, they're pretty rare. But they can add

106

some sparkle to a folktale.

Subsequent theories introduce the possibility that the haunting was a genuine visitation by supernatural entities. Williams-Wynn tells the story this way in her diary entry dated November 15, 1830, but she ultimately rejects it, too. "Mr. L," presumably Henry Bilson Legge, was "a very atrocious libertine," one "aided and abetted in all his evil practices by an old butler named Robin." The sinful Mr. L impregnated his wife's sister (echoes of Cock Lane!), and Robin "destroyed" the child. Somehow, these *four* former residents—*five,* if we include the infant—explain the *three* voices heard by Ricketts. Did the spirits of the mother and child move on to a better place? There's also mention of the "soft aerial music" that matches the "sounds of harmony" in the M.R. chronicle, but exactly how this figures into a scenario about a house haunted by an evil past isn't explained. Perhaps the discontinuity between the ghostly manifestations and this backstory accounts for why, in the end, Williams-Wynn joins Scott and Howard in deciding the haunting was all a deception. She abruptly ends her diary entry by expressing her "utter disbelief of any supernatural agency," adding that the ruse was possibly "to further the purposes of a gang of smugglers." [9] We now have four theories: superstitious self-deception, a gardener perpetrating an elaborate hoax, smugglers doing the same, and the genuine ghosts of former inhabitants driven to haunt the place.

The smuggler theory begs the question of what was it about Hinton Ampner that was worth so much effort. Barham addresses this theory—adding that the smugglers were said to be "aided by the collusion of the servants"—and then he refutes "the latter part of the supposition" by pointing out that the servants were frequently replaced. This is confirmed by Ricketts' diary, "which she had regularly caused all the domestics, as they left her service, to sign. . . ." This only further weakens an already rickety theory.

Earlier, Barham addresses the genuine-ghosts theory, but he says it was a niece, not a sister-in-law, who became pregnant. Ricketts, he says, looked into these rumors. She met with an elderly carpenter who said he had once been hired to "cut out a portion of the planks" in the floor, in which Robin hid a box that "he said contained valuable deeds." Without hesitation, the old workman relocated the spot. Unfortunately, while the marks of his having sawed there remained, the secret box wasn't there. "After this investigation which ended in nothing," writes Barham, "the noises and whisperings, though never distinct, continued with but little diminution, and proved to render the house exceedingly uncomfortable to its inmates."[10] This intriguing clue, then, did nothing to solve the riddle of why the ghosts lingered there.

Neither did tearing down the house to make way for a new one in 1797, though this did seem to end the haunting. As Barham explains, demolishing the place uncovered nothing "to throw any light on the mystery, or to strengthen or refute" the rumors concerning "the crime of Mr. Legg, and the unrest which his spirit, and those of his supposed coadjutor and victim." Another tantalizing yet frustrating clue appeared in the house's rubble. In one of the M.R. chronicle's supplementary documents, labeled "Notes taken by Osborne Markham, Esq., from Mrs. Ricketts's Dictation," we read:

> On being pulled down, there was found by the workmen under the floor of one of the rooms a small skull, said to be that of a monkey; but the matter was never brought forward by any regular inquiry, or professional opinion resorted to as to the real nature of the skull.

Much later, commentators on the case reevaluated this skull. For instance, in 1893, John Crichton-Stuart provided the Society for Psychical Research with a pamphlet version of the M.R. chronicle. Combining it with what peerage records reveal about the house's history, he arrives at a theory mirroring the one involving the previous residents' life of sex and murder. He contends the skull belonged to an unwanted child, adding that it would be "absolutely inexplicable that a monkey's skull should be buried in a small box under the floor of a room."[11] Of course, one might also wonder why the skull of a murdered baby would receive such treatment, too, just as one might wonder why any murderer would dispose of their victim on the premises rather than in, say, a much more isolated and much less incriminating field or lake. (As I say in Chapter One, this element of the Hinton Ampner case fits a tradition of substantiating a haunting by claiming skeletal remains were later found there.)

It might be impossible to find a theory that *perfectly* explains any haunting, but the Hinton Ampner case seems especially difficult to fit into some reasonable framework. Contrast it to some of what we've seen so far: a ghost seeking proper burial of his bones, a squire whose obsession with land persisted after death, a master of the dark arts holding a grudge, and—if not a fraud—a murder victim who sought justice from the Great Beyond. Why couldn't Mary Ricketts—or Jervis, Bolton, and Luttrell—bring their investigations to a satisfying conclusion?

It's because they might well have been confronting a very *different* type of ghost.

Purposeless Ghosts

Ghosts might strike some people as a violation of the natural order. There's birth, then there's life, then there's what's called death, and then—depending on one's faith—there's an afterlife. It's a one-way street, right? Ghosts, however, have either broken the law by backtracking or, perhaps, have been granted divine permission to backtrack.

In fact, it's possible they backtrack as the result of divine commandment. A French monk named Augustin Calmet explains this in his 1746 work, *Dissertations sur les Apparitions des Angels, des Demons & des Espirits,* a historically important study of supernatural entities (especially for those interested in vampires). In a chapter whose title translates to "Difficulties Attending Apparitions," Calmet says that, yes, some ghosts can be attributed to "fraud and illusion, and can be supposed to proceed from the devil only." It's important to differentiate these. Nonetheless, there remains

> a doctrine of the Sorbonne, a school which may justly be styled the first in the Christian world for theological learning, that departed souls do sometimes return to this world, either by the power, or command, or permission of God.

This theological declaration was made in 1518, says Calmet, and repeated "still more expressly" in 1724.[12] The basic notion of ghosts having a divinely sanctioned purpose probably existed well before the Sorbonne made it official.

It certainly reached well beyond the discourse of Catholic theologians in France. The principle pops up in Ann Radcliffe's Gothic novel *A Sicilian Romance,* first published in 1792. When sisters Emilia and Julia confront the daunting possibility of ghosts, Madame de Menon, their governess, instructs them:

> Who shall say that anything is impossible to God? We know that he has made us, who are embodied spirits; he, therefore, can make unembodied spirits. . . . Such spirits, if indeed they have ever been seen, can have appeared only by the express permission of God, and for some very singular purposes; be assured that there are no beings who act unseen by him; and that, therefore,

110

there are none from whom innocence can ever suffer harm.[13]

This makes a ghost hunter's job fairly straightforward. First, determine the authenticity of the ghost. If it's real, determine its purpose for manifesting in the earthly realm. Finally, help the ghost to achieve its aim—or exorcise it, if its purpose is evil. Of course, this is all probably easier said than done.

Some help is afforded from those who have categorized the main reasons ghosts have had for returning to the physical plane. An antiquarian named Francis Grose did exactly this and put it into a handy summary of old and contemporary ghostlore in his 1787 book *A Provincial Glossary, with a Collection of Local Proverbs and Popular Superstitions.* (Its sections on ghosts are reprinted in the Appendix of this book.) Some of what he discusses are matters we've seen earlier: a ghost might appear to identify a murderer or to be reinterred in consecrated ground with proper ceremony. Sometimes, says Grose, a spirit returns "to inform their heir in what secret place, or private drawer in an old trunk, they had hidden the title deeds of the estate," which might've fit the Hinton Ampner case if that box had remained under the floorboards. If the rumors of Legg's sins were valid, the haunting might fit the pattern of ghosts who, "having committed some injustice whilst living, cannot rest till that is redressed." Such cursed souls serve a purpose beyond trying to right a wrong: they provide observable evidence of the terrible punishment awaiting those who stray from the moral path, and Dodge's land-obsessed squire can be made to fit here.

Though he does so very briefly, Grose also mentions a different kind of ghost: those with no apparent purpose. While exploring the curious topic of spectral clothing, he mentions white-clad churchyard ghosts, "who have no particular business, but seem to appear *pro bono publico,* or to scare drunken rustics from tumbling over their graves."[14]

Despite Grose's having a bit of fun with the idea, this comment is a sign of ghosts to come.

Jump to from 1787 to 1885. The Society for Psychical Research published a remarkable article written by Eleanor Sidgwick and titled "Notes on the Evidence, Collected by the Society, for Phantasms of the Dead." In it, she refers to the Society's "collection of about 370 narratives . . . of phenomena, not clearly physical, and which believers in ghosts would be apt to refer to the agency of deceased human beings." Sidgwick narrows these down to the 25 narratives that provide the most reliable evidence for "ascertaining what psychical theories, if any, they seem to point to." Toward the end of the article, she draws eight conclusions, starting by *dismissing* the idea that "ghosts haunt old houses only or even mainly." In addition, there's only slight evidence in support of specters reappearing on significant anniversaries and of a crime or tragedy being connected to the haunting. Sidgwick's next conclusion has particular relevance to us here:

> Fourthly, there is a total absence of any apparent object or intelligent action on the part of the ghost. If its visits have an object, it entirely fails to explain it. It does not communicate important facts. It does not point out lost wills or hidden treasure. It does not even speak, except in the instance mentioned by Mr. Hill, where the ghost replied, 'What is that to you?' to an inquiry; but for this incident there is at best third-hand evidence, and it may have been a mistake.[15]

In sharp contrast to those categorized by Grose a century earlier, the bulk of reports at the Society involved ghosts with no apparent mission and, it seems, no particular interest in communicating with those left behind.

This discovery seems to be what Andrew Lang had in mind when, a few years later, he contrasted the "old-

fashioned ghost" and "the ghost of the nineteenth century."
He explains:

> Readers of the *Proceedings of the Psychical Society* will
> see that the modern ghost is a purposeless creature. He
> appears nobody knows why; he has no message to
> deliver, no secret crime to reveal, no appointment to
> keep, no treasure to disclose, no commission to be
> executed, and, as an almost invariable rule, he does not
> speak, even if you speak to him.

Elsewhere, Lang clarifies that he wasn't suggesting ghosts
had all agreed to become purposeless at some specific point
in the early 1800s. He says:

> The more probable theory is that the old believers in the
> old-fashioned ghost chiefly collected and recorded the
> more striking and interesting cases—those in which the
> ghost showed a purpose (as a few modern ghosts still
> do)—while these anecdotes were, doubtless, improved
> upon and embellished. The early students would
> scarcely think the aimless ghosts worthy of mention,
> though they do mention some of them.[16]

Purposeless ghosts were only background actors in the early
acts, but they took center stage during the 1800s. I sense that
they remain there in the 2000s.

Let me, then, toss out an idea: the Hinton Ampner case
of 1765-1772 illustrates a haunting by ghosts with no clear
aim, no discernable purpose. Essentially, those churchyard
ghosts that Grose said have "no particular business" moved
inside. Any attempt to establish some reason for the manifestations winds up being as frustrating as prying up those
floorboards and finding no deedbox or anything else. Even
Crichton-Stuart's enthusiastic attempt to confirm the rumors
of bygone criminal acts is deemed "incompletely

established" by the journal's editor at the end of the article. Among the problems are the fact that the individual identified as the woman whose baby was murdered would have been over 50 years old when that happened and "[t]he only evidence for connecting the apparitions that were seen with the former inmates of the house is that, in one case out of the four, the apparition was said to have some resemblance" to the man incriminated by Crichton-Stuart.[17] Rather than attempt to make frame Hinton Ampner as some purpose-driven haunting, then, perhaps it should be seen as a purposeless one.

There's a curious observation repeated in those memoirs that substantiate the haunting and Rickett's chronicle of it. When asked about the case, Captain Jervis "not only cut the subject short, but assiduously avoided it," according to Howard. Williams-Wynn says that "he was extremely angry whenever the subject was alluded to," and Barham adds that "the subject was a very sore one to the day of his death."[18] Did the navy-captain-turned-ghost-hunter discover something so distasteful or otherwise upsetting that he refused to discuss it? Another possibility is that he sternly avoided the topic because his week-long investigation was so aggravatingly unresolved—even beyond formulating a *tentative* solution. Put another way, in an era when ghosts were supposed to exhibit some kind of purpose, did the Captain keep quiet because he had been unable to find anything purposeful to report?

Instead of feeling like a failure, though, a ghost hunter who encounters a *purposeless* ghost and identifies it as exactly that can certainly claim success.

[1] The chronicle, with supporting letters and follow-up documents, was published in two parts as "A Hampshire Ghost Story," *Gentleman's Magazine* 233 (November 1872) pp. 547-559 and (December 1872) pp. 666-678.

[2] Walter Scott, *Letters on Demonology and Witchcraft* (John Murray, 1830) pp. 359-360.

[3] Catherine Mary Howard, *Reminiscences for My Children* (Printed for the author by Charles Thurman, 1836) pp. 132-34. Frances Williams-Wynn, *Diaries of a Lady of Quality* (Longman, et al., 1864) pp. 201, 204. Richard Harris Barham, *Life and Letters of Rev. Richard Harris Barham,* vol. 1 (Richard Bently, 1870) p. 306.

[4] All references are to "A Hamphire Ghost Story." To avoid distraction, I have refrained from footnoting every citation in this timeline.

[5] "A Hampshire Ghost Story," p. 678.

[6] Williams-Wynn, p. 203. Barham, p. 307.

[7] Scott, p. 360.

[8] Howard, pp. 133-134.

[9] Williams-Wynn discusses the sinful history on p. 202 and her preference for the smuggler theory on pp. 209-210.

[10] Barham discusses his problems with the smuggler theory on p. 313 and revises the sinful history on pp. 309-311.

[11] While some online sources say 1793, 1797 is the date of demolition given in John Ingram's *The Haunted Homes and Family Traditions of Great Britain* (W.H. Allen, 1884) p. 179. Barham, p. 313-14. "A Hampsire Ghost Story," p. 676. "Cases Received by the Literary Committee," *Journal for the Society of Psychical Research* 6 (April 1893) p. 73.

[12] Augustin Calmet, *Dissertations upon the Apparitions of Angels, Dæmons, and Ghosts,* anonymous translation (Printed for M. Cooper, 1759) pp. 131-132.

[13] Ann Radcliffe, *A Sicilian Romance,* vol. 1 (Printed for Hookham and Carpenter, 1792) pp. 83-84.

[14] Francis Grose, *A Parochial Glossary, with a Collection of Local Proverbs and Popular Superstitions* (Printed for S. Hooper, 1787) pp. 6-7 and 9-10 of the "Superstitions" section.

[15] Mrs. H. Sidgwick, "Notes on the Evidence, Collected by the Society, for Phantasms of the Dead," *Proceedings of the Society for Psychical Research* 3 (April 24, 1885) pp. 70-71, 142-143.

[16] Andrew Lang, *Cock Lane and Common-sense* (Longmans, Green, and Co., 1894) p. 95. Andrew Lang, "Ghosts up to Date," *Blackwood's* 155 (January 1894) p. 52.

[17] "Cases Received by the Literary Committee," pp. 73-74.

[18] Howard, p. 133. Williams-Wynn, p. 209. Barham, p. 313.

CHAPTER SIX

A POETIC INTERLUDE

Search the roads of Dublin, Ireland—either in person or on a map—and look for Railway Street. It runs east-west, parallel to and between Sean MacDermott Street Lower to the north and Foley to the south. Now, imagine Railway extending west to reach Marlborough Street by barreling through the buildings and across the grounds of the present day. This extended version of Railway is where Mecklenburgh Street ran back in 1785.

That's the year when a woman living somewhere along Mecklenburgh claimed to have been visited by a ghost. The unnamed woman's troubles—and a ghost hunter's night in the haunted house—were reported in *The Hibernian Magazine,* which was published in Dublin.[1] The story of the spectral visitation starts with an image that feels a bit like something from Dickens' *A Christmas Carol* (1843).

The woman opened her eyes. Someone was opening the curtains around her bed! Though it was dark, she perceived a stranger. It was a female form, one dressed in sable robes. The form's face was unfamiliar, but the expression was of a woman bearing a heavy burden.

That would have been upsetting enough, but this stranger was also "surrounded by an illumination like lightning," according to the *Hibernian* article. This, then, was no ordinary woman. It was some kind of supernatural phantom—and it was beckoning the

117

drowsy woman to *follow.*

But, no, she did not have the courage to follow.

The next day, the haunted resident told her relatives about the encounter, and she was apparently convincing enough that two of them agreed to sleep with her the next night. They, too, encountered the ghost, though this time it announced its presence with "groans and uncommon noises." They grew terrified, too, so much so that they were unable to attempt any investigation of the apparition or those sounds.

The woman said—and even swore—that she *knew* the ghost was there to do her harm. Given her relatives' confirmation of the visitation, she fled the house to stay with neighbors. In a way, she acted like those who, centuries earlier, had been frightened away from the haunted house in Greece before Athenodorus arrived.

Word of the visitation traveled, and soon crowds filled Mecklenburgh Street in the hope of witnessing this bizarre manifestation. At some point, a man the *Hibernian* describes as "Mr. Nolan, so well known for his poetical and political abilities," accepted a dare. He agreed to be locked within the haunted house for one night by himself. Well, he wasn't entirely alone. Nolan brought a dog along with a pair of pistols on the chance that something criminal was lurking behind the haunting. Like Athenodorus, he also brought implements to do some writing.

Unlike Athenodorus, though, this ghost hunter didn't unearth any startling secret. "Suffice it to say," reports the *Hibernian,* Nolan "saw no ghost, though he heard many noises, and loudly threatened to shoot the first who should approach him, whether of this world or the other." This silenced the noises, and the citizens of Mecklenburgh Street "have since got rid of their fears in the neighborhood." So effective was Nolan's threat that he was found fast asleep in the morning, a candle and the room's fire having both extinguished themselves.

Given this undramatic finale, the haunting and Nolan's night on Mecklenburgh Street might not have been quite interesting enough to make the pages of the *Hibernian* or any other publication. However, remember that the poetic politician had brought writing tools: paper along with a feather quill and an inkwell or perhaps a pencil made of leather-wrapped graphite. At some point during his nocturnal surveillance, Nolan completed a poem. Fittingly, this work is a meditation on ghosts, the misguided fear of them, and how wonderful it would be if the great and noble dead were allowed to revisit the world. The ghost hunter's productive use of his otherwise lackluster adventure gave the story a unique twist and a life lesson about using one's time wisely.

The article about the Mecklenburgh Street mystery and how Nolan ended it—without solving it—attracted widespread attention for decades. Here's a list of when and where I've found it reprinted after appearing in Dublin in 1785:

> 1792: London
> 1792: Philadelphia
> 1793: Glasgow
> 1793: Edinburgh
> Circa 1800: Preston, England
> 1802: London
> 1811: London
> 1815: Boston, Massachusetts
> 1817: Newcastle upon Tyne
> 1826: New York[2]

Keep in mind that this ghost story traveled before the telegraph was invented and the railroads were built. It very likely crossed the Atlantic by sail, not steam. And my list is just a sampling.

However, the appeal of the report did not rest solely on the facts presented. At the end of the *Hibernian* article and each of those reprints listed, Nolan's poem is presented. In fact, perhaps because it was so frequently reprinted, that poem seems to have outlived the poet's fame. With no mention of who wrote them, the opening lines appear in an 1851 article about Sir Thomas More and, oddly enough, in an 1864 book about geology and paleontology.[3] Here, then, is the ultimate attraction of this case: a poem about ghosts that was written by a ghost hunter during a ghost hunt.

A Ghost Hunter's Poem

Before sharing the poem itself, bear with me long enough to clarify a few words and names found in it. First, "cerements" refers to the shroud wrapped around a corpse for burial, and "adamantine" means unyielding and extremely strong. Socrates is easily recognized as the esteemed Greek philosopher, but less so is Titus, a respected Roman emperor. Nolan clearly admired the Classical Greeks and Romans, placing them far above the Vandals, a people remembered for having plundered Gaul (now France and Belgium), Spain, northern Africa, and Rome.

Closer to home, James Burgh (1714–1775) was a Scot who argued for free speech, religious tolerance, and universal suffrage. His two-volume *Political Disquisitions* was prized by revolutionary thinkers such as Thomas Jefferson and John Adams. Closer still, David La Touche (1703-1785) was a Dubliner who presided over one of that city's most successful banks. He and his family were famous for their charity, and he died the month before the poem was first published.[4] At the time, La Touche might have been very much in the thoughts of Nolan and Dublin readers.

Here, then, is Nolan's poem:

Stanzas Written in a Haunted Room

If from the cerements of the silent dead
Our long-departed friends could rise anew,
    Why feel a horror, or conceive a dread,
To see again those friends which once we knew?
      To gaze on Beauty's melancholy shade?
      Or hear the sorrow of the lovelorn maid?

    Father of all! thou gave *not* to our ken,
To view beyond the ashes of our grave;
    'Tis not the idle tales of busy men
That can the soul appall. The truly brave,
      Seated on reason's adamantine throne,
      Can place the soul, and fears no ills unknown.

    O! if the flinty prison of the grave
Could loose its doors, and let the spirit flee,
    Why not return the wise, the just, the brave,
And set, once more, the pride of ages free?
      Why not restore a Socrates again?
      Or give thee, Titus, as the first of men?

    Dear friends of humankind! you cannot come
To mend the manners of a Vandal age;
    Lost are the best of Athens and of Rome,
Nor patriot chief remains, nor hoary sage;
      Intombed in dark oblivion's cave they lie
      Strangers to all the fame of round Eternity.

    In this lone room where yet I patient wait,
To try if souls departed can appear,
    O! could a Burgh escape his prison gate,
Or could I think La Touche's form was near!
      Why fear to view the shades which long must be
      Sacred to Freedom and to Charity?

A little onward in the path of life,
And all must stretch in death their mortal frame,
A few short struggles end the weary strife,
And blot the frail memorial of our name.
Torn from the promontory's lofty brow,
In time, the rooted oak itself lies low.

Nolan never takes a firm position on the reality of ghosts in this poem. He wonders what *if* our dead friends could return and what *if* the door back from the grave were open, and he says he conducted the ghost hunt to find out *if* souls can return. This iffy-ness gives the poem a contemplative feel. It reflects a mental meandering through the murky uncertainties of ghosts, never forgetting the crystal-clear certainty of death.

One way to approach this poem is to see it as a dialog. This dialog might occur between two completely distinct characters—or between two voices in a single brain, as if someone is going back and forth while contemplating ghosts. The voice in the odd numbered stanzas (meaning those groups of lines separated by spaces) is inventive and hopeful. It's inquisitive, too, as shown by the questions asked in the first, third, and fifth stanzas. The voice in the even numbered stanzas, on the other hand, replies to those questions in a very down-to-earth and sort of melancholy manner.

In the first stanza, for instance, the inquisitive voice asks something like: "Assuming ghosts are real, doesn't it make more sense to *welcome* them rather than fear them?" The second stanza shrugs its shoulders and replies: "Don't bother asking. God prevents access to the Afterlife, so the point is moot. Brave and rational people aren't taken in by made-up ghost stories." The line about the brave, sitting on the throne of Reason, being able to "place the soul" is interesting. It probably refers to the long history of philosophical debates about where the soul exists in the physical body. For example, in a 1733 essay titled "Of the Power of Spirits to Move Bodies, of Their Being in a Place and Removing from It," Isaac Watts asks how the soul, "tho' it be supposed to have its chief residence in the brain," is able to reach far enough to control the limbs—even "tho' your Philosophy should place the Soul never so close to them."[5] Nolan adapts such language to suggest that clear-headed people know that the souls of the departed have *departed* and gone to a better place. Or maybe a worse place.

The question-answer pattern is repeated twice more. The third stanza shows the more imaginative voice wondering about the good that would come if Socrates could share more of his wisdom or Titus could return to advise the living on leadership. This dream is squashed, however, in the fourth stanza with a lament about how such ghostly guidance would be wasted on the lowly brutes who followed those greats. The fifth stanza offers a compromise by rephrasing the question with admirable men who died much more recently: "Why should we be afraid of ghosts like Burgh and La Touche?" The sixth stanza ends the conversation by bluntly suggesting: "Look, everyone dies. *Everyone!* Deal with it." This last stanza strikes me as sidestepping the question before it, but maybe Nolan was sleepy at this point. It still serves as a solid conclusion, though.

Speaking of conclusions, I'll end this chapter on a somewhat tangential note. Burgh and La Touche were relatively easy for me to track down. Unfortunately, I've only found teasing clues about who "Mr. Nolan" was.[6] If his ghost ever materializes to lend me a hand in identifying him, I'll do my very best to *not* "feel a horror, or conceive a dread."

[1] "The Story of the Mecklenburgh-street Ghost," *Hibernian Magazine* (March 1785) p. 116.

[2] "A Dublin Anecdote," *A Second Volume of Amusing Anecdotes, Bon-Mots, and Characteristic Traits,* edited by J. Adams (Printed for C. and G. Kearsley, 1792) pp. 77-79. "A Dublin Anecdote," *Gazette of the United States,* November 7, 1792, issue p. 4/volume p. 184. "The Haunted House," *The Phoenix* 2 (April 10, 1793) pp. 219-221. "An Anecdote," *The Bee* 17 (October 2, 1793) pp. 182-183. "The Ghost," *The Union Miscellany; or, Elegant Extracts in Miniature* (Printed by T. Croft, c. 1800) pp. 113-115. "Anecdote of the Celebrated Mr. Nolan: with Observations on the Passion of Fear," *Universal Magazine* 111 (December 1802) pp. 423-425. *The Gleaner: A Series of Periodical Essays,* edited by Nathan Drake, vol. 4 (Printed for Suttaby, Evance, and Co., 1811) pp. 124-127. "Stanzas Written in a Haunted Room," *The Boston Spectator* 1 (February 11, 1815) p. 236. "The Ghost Laid," *The Woman's Guide to Virtue, Economy, and Happiness,* edited by John Armstrong (Printed by MacKenzie and Dent, 1817) pp. 430-31. "Mr. Nolan," *The New-York Mirror* 3 (June 17, 1826) pp. 373-374.

[3] A.M. [Anne Manning], "Sir Thomas More and Erasmus," *Sharpe's London Journal* 14 (1851) p. 240. J.L. Milton, *The Stream of Life on Our Globe* (Robert Hardwicke, 1864) p. 390.

[4] On Burgh's influence, see Oscar and Mary Handlin's "James Burgh and American Revolutionary Thought," *Proceedings of the Massachusetts Historical Society* 73 (1961) pp. 38-57. On the La Touche family's generosity, see their entry in David C.A. Agnew's *Protestant Exiles from France, Chiefly in the Reign of Louis XIV,* vol. 2 (For Private Circulation, 1886) pp. 404-405. On the death date—February 20, 1785—see C. MacCarthy Tenison's "The Old Dublin Bankers, VI: La Touche's Bank," *Journal of the Institue of Bankers in Ireland* 4 (July 1902) p. 198.

[5] Issac Watts, *Philosophical Essays on Various Subjects* (Printed for Richard Ford, 1733) pp. 153-154. The history of the search for the soul in the body is a fascinating one, reaching back at least as far as the ancient Egyptians.

[6] One clue to the poet's identity appears in a book of poems by Egan O'Rahilly, where there's a reference to a privately owned "collection of Irish poems and tales," most of which were written before 1800 and some of which were written by a John O'Nolan. See *Dánta Aoðagáin Uí Raiaille: The Poems of Egan O'Rahilly,* edited by Patrick S. Dinneen (Irish Texts Society, 1900) p. lviii. Another clue is found accompanying the New York Public Library's collection titled "Old Irish manuscripts," which is cataloged as "[t]ranscribed by John O'Nolan (Seaghn O'Nulain),

a minor Irish poet who flourished at the end of the 18th and beginning of the 19th centuries." See "Guide to the Old Irish manuscripts, undated, MssCol 1774," *The New York Public Library Manuscripts and Archives Division.* PDF file. https://archives.nypl.org/mss/1774. I bow to any researcher who can identify this poetic Irish ghost hunter, be he John O'Nolan or someone else.

CHAPTER SEVEN

A FATAL GHOST HUNT:
FRANCIS SMITH
ON BLACK LION LANE

At the start of the 1800s, ghost hunting changed in two important ways. First, the term itself had become common enough that it began to appear in newspapers with no added clarification of the meaning. It was probably familiar enough in *spoken* language that readers would have understood it. Second, the practice of ghost hunting earned a very negative reputation. On January 3, 1804, Francis Smith, aged 29, shot and killed Thomas Millwood, aged 22, on Black Lion Lane in London's Hammersmith district. On the surface, Smith's primary reason for detaining Millwood and then pulling the trigger was the latter wore the white outfit of his profession, a bricklayer. Smith was acting as one of a group that the press called "ghost-hunters,"[1] and Millwood's white clothing made him look something like a ghost.

Of course, there are questions surrounding the killing. What had inspired Smith to conduct nocturnal surveillance on the streets that night? Why was he armed? Did he think he was stalking a genuine ghost or intending to apprehend a hoaxer? When Smith had Millwood at gunpoint—the bricklayer apparently doing nothing more threatening than refusing to identify himself—why did that gun discharge? We'll explore these questions, arriving at possible answers.

For now, here are the facts of the case, taken from newspaper reports published throughout the week after the shooting and from the transcript of the trial, which was held only eight days later.

During the final weeks of 1803, Londoners walking the streets of the Hammersmith district after dark were being harassed by a ghost. To be fair, it was probably someone *dressed up* like a ghost. Exactly what was happening is hard to sort out, and the newspapers commented on the swirl of exaggerations and rumors. The *St. James's Chronicle* explained that the neighborhood was being "alarmed by some idle or ill-disposed person, who assumed the fancied appearance of a ghost," and that the costumed culprit, "according to some, appeared in the likeness of [Napoleon] Bonaparte; according to others, of a horse without a head; but the fact is, to all that really saw it, it was a tall figure in a white sheet." In a later article, the *Chronicle* added that some said the ghost had eyes "like a *glow worm*—others, that he *breathed fire and smoke*—and others again, that he vanished in a moment, and sunk in the earth in their presence!" A competing newspaper called the *Star* stood up for ethical journalism, declaring: "We shall not repeat the numerous ridiculous tales that are circulated." The actions of the "ghost" must have been far from silly, though, because both papers say that the residents of Hammersmith were panicking and often too fearful to venture out.[2] Quite likely, the exaggerations and rumors only raised the level of fear.

One of the persistent claims made about the "ghost's" wrongdoings involves a pregnant woman. The *Star* reported that she crossed paths with the sheeted figure and "was so much shocked at this supposed ghost, that she took to her bed, where she still lies in great danger." This incident was also reported in the *Chronicle,* but with additional, possibly dubious, details. The woman met the "ghost" in a churchyard, where it rose from the tombstones. "She attempted to run," according to this version, "but the ghost soon overtook her, and pressing her in his arms, she fainted." Some neighbors found her still unconscious, took her home and put her to bed, but "alas! she never rose." This implication that the woman died was made blatant a decade later, when an editor chose this version for a book of shocking crime stories. Next, in an updated edition of the same book a decade after that, the scene of the woman fleeing the "ghost" remained and was even illustrated with the caption: "The pretended Hammersmith Ghost frightening a poor Woman to death."[3] It became a dramatic moment in how the case would be remembered.

Less poignant but just as enduring is the story of a wagoner, a sort of pre-electric trolley driver, who had a brush with the "ghost." Apparently, his eight horses remained calm and the sixteen passengers stayed in their seats, but "the driver took to his heels, and left wagon and horses so precipitately that the whole were greatly endangered." This comes again from the *Star,* which then took a moment to uphold its reputation: "The Ghost . . . was not so very mischievous as to cut the harness of the horses, as erroneously stated in some of the other papers."[4] The story is also repeated by the editors of one and two decades afterward, but they do not repeat the stuff about the harness being damaged.

Yet another encounter with the "ghost" was related at Smith's trial. In fact, it's recorded in the transcript, and it provides a rare, firsthand account. Thomas Groom, an employee at a local brewery, testified:

I was going through the churchyard between eight

and nine o'clock, with my jacket under my arm and my hands in my pocket, when some person came from behind a tombstone . . . and caught me fast by the throat with both hands, and held me fast. My fellow-servant, who was going on before, hearing me scuffling, asked what was the matter; then, whatever it was gave me a twist round, and I saw nothing. I gave a bit of a push out with my fist, and felt something soft, like a great coat.

Presumably, Groom had also related his encounter at the coroner's inquest, prompting the ever-wary *Star* to jeer: "It will hardly be believed that a stout drayman [a brewery delivery person] was collared by the Ghost as he was crossing the churchyard, and, though a very athletic man, was so frightened that he made no resistance, but ran off as fast as he could, roaring for help."[5] It's tough to say how *anyone* would react to being grabbed by the throat after dark. Nonetheless, assuming there's at least a grain of truth in one or two of these encounters, it becomes clear that whoever was "playing ghost" really wasn't playing around.

There's little wonder, then, that a reward for £10 was offered for apprehending the hoaxer. This, combined with the promise of adventure and perhaps some measure of civic duty, inspired several young men to get their guns and patrol the grounds. It's doubtful these lads, dubbed "ghost hunters," thought they were stalking a genuine ghost—they were probably out to *debunk* the haunting. To do so, they relied on two traditional tools of ghost hunting: nocturnal surveillance and patience. Their primary focus was Black Lion Lane (a street that still exists) because this very dark spot, perfect for eluding capture, was where the "ghost" had been known to lurk.[6]

One of these men was Francis Smith, whose day job

was excise officer. He did not act alone exactly. About 10:30 p.m. on Tuesday, January 3, Smith informed William Girdler, a watchman hired by Hammersmith residents, of his intent to foil the "ghost" by staying hidden near Black Lion Lane. According to his testimony, Girdler had agreed to join Smith after completing his usual rounds. The two even agreed on a spoken sign to identify one another: "We agreed, if we met in the lane, to say who comes there? Friend. Advance, friend."[7] It seems Smith wasn't acting *entirely* recklessly.

Yet he still might have been anxious and—worse than that, given the circumstances—eager. As we know, he was definitely armed. Within an hour, he would take Thomas Millwood's life.

You see, the victim's wife still hadn't returned home from her place of employment. The testimony given by Ann Millwood, Thomas's sister, provides a good account of the victim's actions that night. Between 10 and 11 o'clock, Thomas arrived at his parents' residence on Black Lion Lane, where Ann lived, too. He said that he had been to see his wife, but she wouldn't be home for half an hour, and Ann agreed to sit up with him until that time. Around 11:00, as their parents were going to bed, the sister told her brother he'd better go meet his wife and accompany her safely home. After some hesitation, Thomas agreed and said goodnight.

Almost no time had passed after that when Ann heard someone out on Black Lion Lane yell, *"Damn you—who are you, and what are you? Damn you—I will shoot you!"* She continues:

I saw the flash of fire from the gun. I went from the door and called *Thomas* as loud as I could, three or four times, but nobody answered. I went to my mother and said, 'I *do* think my brother is shot!' I

130

did not stay for an answer, but went up to my father, who was in bed, and said, *"Do* get up, for my brother is shot!" He would not believe me. . . . I went to the window and called *Thomas* as loud as I could call. At last, I said, well, if nobody will believe me, I will go myself.

Ann went outside and headed in the direction of Thomas's house. She came upon the fallen body of her brother. Stooping to take his hand, she begged him to speak to her.

But Thomas Millwood was dead.[8]

Shortly beforehand, a clearly upset Smith came upon John Locke, a nearby wine merchant with whom Smith was friendly. He admitted to Locke he had shot the person he thought was pretending to be a ghost. The pair, along with Girdler and another man, went to check the body. Locke testified that "it appeared to be shot on the lower part of the jaw on the left side." A previously published article on the coroner's inquest gives more detail: "The shot had entered [Millwood's] left jaw, which it had totally lacerated, and perforated every part of the head. The piece was fired so close to the deceased, that the skin of his face was totally black." It's reasonable to conclude Smith had panicked, but any flaw in his aim was corrected by his closeness to Millwood.

From here, Smith followed Locke's advice and went home. Meanwhile, the other men contacted officials. Those officials, then, arrived at Smith's residence and took him into custody on suspicion of murder. He went with them without resistance.[9] Apparently, by then, Smith grasped that he had done something terrible.

Justice was swift, but so was mercy. The shooting occurred on a Tuesday, the inquest leading to a charge of murder was held on Thursday, and Smith was in court and found guilty of that crime the following Wednesday. His execution was ordered, but—before the end of the month—this sentence was commuted. Smith "was pardoned on condition of being imprisoned one year," according to the *Chronicle,* and he served only that single year in prison.[10] One is left to wonder how Millwood's wife, sister, and parents reacted to such mercy.

What about whoever was masquerading as a ghost and creating havoc for weeks? Shortly after the shooting, a man confessed. The *Sun* opened the news article by saying that the ghost, "to the satisfaction of the inhabitants of [Hammersmith], has at last been discovered." A shoemaker named Graham admitted to the Magistrate that "he had done it in order to be revenged on the impertinence of his apprentices, who had terrified his children by telling them stories of ghosts." He dressed up as a ghost to scare those workers "as they passed homeward."[11] Unfortunately, this confession is hard to reconcile with a neighborhood in panic for weeks, including reports of a pregnant women grabbed, a wagoner terrified, and a drayman strangled. Unless Graham went far beyond targeting his apprentices once or twice, this solution to the mystery has to be seriously questioned. If Hammersmith residents truly were satisfied with it, they were looking for an easy answer.

Still, no *better* answer was ever found.

We'll never truly comprehend what flashed through Smith's mind the seconds before he pulled the trigger. Was he convinced he had found the right man, and did he suddenly sense the threat posed by a man reputed to be very capable of violent acts? On the stand, the best Smith could do to explain that moment was to stammer:

I did not know what I did. Speaking to the deceased twice, and he not answering, I was so much agitated, I did not know what I did. I solemnly declare my innocence, and that I had no intention to take away the life of the unfortunate deceased, or any other man whatever.[12]

This raises the question: was it Millwood's *not answering* that ignited Smith's reaction?

And the question after that becomes why did Millwood remain silent in such a dangerous situation? Ann Millwood's testimony confirms Smith's claim that Thomas said nothing to answer the demand that he identify who and what he was. There are signs that the bricklayer had a defiant streak. At the trial, a Mrs. Fulbrook was called to the witness stand. She is identified as "related by marriage to the deceased" in the transcript and as his mother-in-law in the *Chronicle*. She explained that Thomas had gone out dressed in his work clothes on a previous occasion. A stranger passed him, one who "dared to say there goes the ghost." Thomas responded by threatening to repay the comment with "a punch of the head." Fulbrook says she then begged her son-in-law to put on an overcoat to avoid similar trouble.[13] Clearly, though, Thomas ignored this heartfelt advice.

These are only glimmers of what happened that night. There's too little to work with to delve into the psychological states of either Smith or Millwood. There's much more evidence for a sociological analysis of the prevailing opinions on ghosts in England as the 1700s turned to the 1800s. Taking this approach illuminates the pressures on and conflicts within, not just these two men, but also a far-ranging population. In turn, this begins to explain what happened on that deadly night.

A Campaign to End Believing in Ghosts

As grisly as it sounds, shortly after the shooting, Millwood's body was taken to the Black Lion Inn—and it remained there until the inquest, which was held in the same place. A pre-trial jury was quickly assembled, and the coroner expressed his thoughts on their decision about what should be done with Smith. As reported in the *Star,* the coroner said that he

> regretted that, in this enlightened age, the fatal event which had convened them should have exhibited such a proof of the superstition of the uninformed part of the community. He had hoped the lights of reason and philosophy would have precluded the possibility of such an injury, but as the experience of the present instance showed that the prejudices and prepossessions of ignorance still prevailed, it was necessary to have distinctly understood that no idea of a ghost justified any person to arm himself with a weapon for the purpose of destroying the supposed apparition.

The jury must have agreed because, "without a moment's hesitation," they decided Smith should be tried for murder.[14] The contrast here between *enlightened/reason* and *uninformed/ignorance* is key, and the coroner was far from alone in using these opposites to shame people into *not* believing in ghosts.

Perhaps not surprisingly, another authoritative source rallying against such belief was science—specifically, medical science. A year after the coroner addressed the jurors at the Black Lion Inn, John Alderson, M.D., made a speech to "a Literary and Philosophical Society at Hull." Alderson related his experiences with a patient who, after a head injury, was "tormented with a variety of spectres, sometimes of people who had been long dead, and other

134

times of friends who were living." The psychological haunting "was effectually removed by bleeding with leeches, and active purgatives." Another patient was a gout-ridden elderly woman who "suffered, for many days and nights together, the intrusion of a variety of phantoms," including those of "friends long lost." Again, a medical remedy stopped the hallucinations: "cataplasms to the feet, and gentle purgatives." A third patient was plagued by apparitions—not of the dead—but of "transatlantic friends" and family he had left behind in America. As with the others, this man was otherwise rational and sane, and his malady vanished, too.

Had his patients remained uncured of the physical ailments causing their delusions—or had they witnessed phantoms on a single occasion or only at night—Alderson says that "no power on earth would ever have altered their opinion" that they had met genuine ghosts. From this, the doctor concludes that *all* perceptions of ghosts, across the globe and through the ages, are rooted, "not in the perturbed spirits of the departed, but in the diseased organization of the living." This speech was then published in the *Edinburgh Medical and Surgical Journal* in 1810, and it was revised for an 1823 pamphlet. In time, Alderson was joined by other physicians interested in similar hallucinatory symptoms who also traced them to physiological or psychological maladies.[15] Of course, correctly attributing *three*—or even *three thousand*—cases of people believing they had encountered a ghost to an underlying medical cause hardly explains away *all* such cases. Nonetheless, as science continued to affirm that human perception was unreliable under certain conditions, the notion that ghosts were a trick of the mind was given scientific support.

In fact, even people without head injuries, gout, or transatlantic friends could be tricked into perceiving ghosts, and they paid money for exactly that experience. With roots reaching back to the 1500s, a device called a magic lantern used mirrors and maybe a puff or two of smoke to fabricate apparitions. Audiences paid to witness the effect, and by the time of the Hammersmith ghost case, such acts had become polished. Historian Owen Davies explains that, in the late 1700s, magic lantern technology took a leap forward with rear-screen projection, which hid the apparatus from the audience while allowing the operator projecting the ghostly images literally to leap forward. "Moving the lantern backwards and forward in synchronization with an adjustable diaphragm built into the lantern's optical tube produced the startling effect of ghosts lunging towards the audience and then receding," he explains, adding that acts featuring the improved equipment crossed the English Channel to play in London in 1801.[16]

At first glance, such entertainment would only subtly imply that there's no such thing as *real* ghosts by showing that apparitions can be manufactured. Did these shows have any influence on the audience's attitudes toward ghosts witnessed *outside* the theater? They were certainly marketed to do so. An 1802 notice for one show promises to display "phantoms or apparitions of the dead or absent in a way more illusive than has ever been presented to the eye of the public." The ad ends by stating that the show is designed "to open the eyes of those who still foster an absurd belief in ghosts or disembodied spirits," with the added benefit of providing "pleasing entertainment."[17] Whether or not anyone in the audience was *actually* persuaded to drop their spectral convictions is another matter.

Stage shows weren't the only form of entertainment aimed at eradicating such beliefs. I have discussed in previous chapters how Ann Radcliffe gained surprising popularity by writing novels in which characters shake and shiver at what appear to be supernatural mysteries—only to then discover natural solutions to them. Joseph Taylor might have had Radcliffe's success in mind as he was organizing his 1814 anthology featuring spooky stories with "rationalized" endings. Whether the misleading hauntings are revealed to be cases of sleepwalking, ventriloquism, schoolboy pranks, or something else, Taylor drew his material from anecdotes he had heard personally as well as "from history and respectable publications." He says the tales were chosen to "not only entertain, but likewise convince the *thinking* part of mankind of the absurdity in believing every silly tale without first tracing the promulgation to its source." Between the introduction and the ghost stories sits an essay by Taylor, and if his authorial agenda wasn't blatant enough, this piece begins: "There is no folly more predominant, in the country at least, than a ridiculous and superstitious fear of ghosts and apparitions."[18] Storytelling can certainly be an appealing and powerful method to teach a lesson, and writers such as Radcliffe and Taylor probably had some influence on readers.

Expository essays influence readers, too, and essayists had been teaching the same lesson for decades. Published in 1764, William Shenstone's "An Opinion of Ghosts" opens (after casting a few aspersions at Catholicism) by saying that ghosts are products of "the defects of the imagination." Those embroiled in liquor, terror, fever, lunacy, "or even walking in their sleep, have had their brain as deeply impressed with chimerical representations." Such nightmare images become fixed "with the same force as their eyes themselves could have portrayed them." Once this has happened, ghosts multiply, spurred on by grief and guilt felt for the deceased. Shenstone concludes by claiming that such illusive spectral encounters are decreasing and goes so far as saying that ghosts "have not been reported to have appeared these twenty years." The trend can continue, he assures readers, by putting "a strict guard over our passions . . . and by making frequent appeals to cool reason and common-sense."[19] To sum up Shenstone's opinion, ghosts are a matter of psychological delusion, but they can be eradicated with mental discipline.

Yet the belief in ghosts continued, and questions of a more religious nature surrounded them. A year after the Hammersmith tragedy, John Bigland addressed the spirituality of spirits in a sequence of essays. Not a fan of the soft sell, Bigland states: "The doctrine of ghosts and apparitions, . . . when contemplated with the eye of reason, merits only to be treated with ridicule, contempt, and disregard." He then takes on those who "imagine that a disbelief of apparitions is a mark of irreligion and impiety," and who argue: "Nothing is impossible with God." Ghosts, replies Bigland, *are* impossible, given God's goodness and wisdom. After an examination of scripture, he explains that a spirit appearing to "mortal eyes" constitutes a miracle, and "both reason and revelation teach us that it is inconsistent with the Supreme Being, and derogatory to his glory, to alter the established laws of nature for trifling and capricious purposes." From there, Bigland shifts to attributing ghosts to "the disordered imaginations of those who fancy they see them," and he nods to Shenstone along the way.[20] One might ask who made up the readership of Bigland or Shenstone. It was probably those with the education and leisure to find such learned discourse of value.

However, the same basic message was aimed at a greater range of readers. For example, *The Young Woman's Guide to Virtue, Economy, and Happiness* is introduced as intended for marriageable women and female servants. Combining tips on etiquette, home economics, minor medical remedies, cookery, and even brewing malt liquor and making wine, this instructional manual was published in 1817 and compiled by John Armstrong. That's right—684 pages of guidance for women from a man. Lurking among all that advice is a section titled "On Apparitions," and there Armstrong says that belief in supernatural entities stirs "the most ungrounded and agonizing fears, which in women are sometimes the cause of very serious and even fatal consequences." He seems to nod to the tales told by Taylor when explaining that

> many extraordinary [spectral] appearances, which have created great alarm, have been afterwards completely accounted for; from which there is reason to believe that all the rest might, however improbable they appeared at the time, be reduced to some natural combination of circumstances. Hence it is that among a civilized people, and particularly those whose judgments are enlightened and correct, a credulous belief in events contrary to the common course of nature is almost unknown.[21]

Refusing to believe in ghosts, according to Armstrong's instruction, was one way for a young woman to be happy, virtuous—and not dead.

Armstrong might have been hoping to catch his readers too late in their lives. Other writers targeted children. In 1791, Mary Weightman introduced children to Caroline, a happy skeptic, and her sad and fearful friends, Matilda and Henrietta, in *The Friendly Monitor: or, Dialogues for Youth Against the Fear of Ghosts, and Other Irrational Apprehensions, with Reflections on the Power of the Imagination and the Folly of Superstition.* Caroline challenges her friends' beliefs by raising questions about how ghosts are "capable of removing the mass of earth that is universally thrown over every poor corpse" and about "their dress being the very same they wore when alive." In 1819, Frances Maria MacDonald took a decidedly religious approach to accomplish the same in *Twenty-Four Sermons, Calculated for Children, and Explanatory of the Essential Doctrines of Christianity.* She tells her young audience that, while the Bible includes some examples of people reappearing after death, such miracles no longer occur. In fact, "on the contrary, it is perfectly inconsistent with the goodness and mercy of God, to suppose that he would allow of such things, merely to frighten people."[22] In terms of influence, such works targeted at children were most likely formidable.

I could go on. I hope, though, that I've shown that physicians, stage magicians, storytellers, essayists, and advisors for young women and small children were acting independently in a far-ranging campaign to demolish Britain's belief in ghosts. Spanning science and religion, spoken and written language, young and mature readers, the campaign almost certainly had *some* impact on the British population in the late 1700s and early 1800s.

While the campaign failed to achieve *complete* success, it seems to have changed ghost hunting in at least one singular and striking way: ghost hunters began to make space for *guns* in their overnight bags.

A Gallery of Ghost Hunters with Guns

In an era when serious doubts were cast on the reality of ghosts, a ghost hunter was at least as much a debunker as a paranormal investigator. If one assumed there might be a hoaxer at work—possibly someone committing a crime and/or capable of violence if caught—having a gun ready was prudent. As discussed in the last chapter, Mr. Nolan knew this when he investigated the 1785 Mecklenburgh Street haunting, and so he packed a pair of pistols along with his writing gear.

However, the story of the ghost-hunting poet was not the only one readers in Hammersmith might have read or heard, and in turn, Francis Smith's exploits added to a narrative tradition that continued after it. Here is a sampling of narratives, both factual and fictional, illustrating how ghost hunting was being transformed both in practice and in the public imagination. As one century became the next, some ghost hunters included firearms. (The years in bold indicate when the narrative was published, not when the narrated events occurred.)

1782: In his memoirs, a career soldier named Peter Henry Bruce shares an anecdote set during the Russo-Persian War (1722-1723). One night, Bruce dined with the local governor. This official told "a long story about a ghost that was frequently seen walking the streets at night, and had continued to do so for some years past, bestowing a sound beating on any person who offered to disturb it, but did no other harm." Bruce asked why no one had apprehended the so-called "ghost," but the governor, "who was a very credulous man," pooh-poohed such skepticism. The military man offered to perform that task, which the governor "granted with a sneer." Bruce and some of the men in his battalion promptly tracked down and seized the culprit, and once Bruce "presented a pistol to his breast, he begged to save his life." He was a Cossack, who then received "a severe whipping, after he stood for some time with his white sheet around him, as a show to the people of the town."[23]

1785: Mr. Nolan investigated the Mecklenburgh Street haunting.

1794: In Elizabeth Gunning's novel *The Packet,* Sir William interviews those who claim to have witnessed a specter at the local church. Remaining skeptical, he promises to investigate. "With a brace of pistols in his pocket and sword under his arm, followed by his own man, whom [a worried friend] would not have left out of the ghost-hunting party," Sir William sets out to conduct nocturnal surveillance at the church. In the end, the gun proves unnecessary, for things are *not as they seem!*[24]

1799: *Walpoliana* is a collection of anecdotes and other remarks from the pen and mouth of Horace Walpole, the same man who had disapproved of the treatment of Elizabeth Parsons on Cock Lane. One of the tales there involves a haunted castle in Hardivillers, France. The site was riddled by strange noises, weird flames, and multiple apparitions, making it so fearful that only a farmer hired to act as caretaker could tolerate it. The owner was "obliged to let the estate to the farmer at a very low rent."

After some time, though, the owner and two of his friends decided to conduct nocturnal surveillance, "and if any noise or apparitions disturbed them, to discharge their pistols at either sound or ghost." On their first night, they heard a rattling of chains upstairs. There, in a chamber filled with smoke, the investigators discovered a figure with horns and a tail! A chase began, and one of the investigators "discharged his pistol at [the devilish figure's] back, and hit him exactly in the middle, but was himself seized with fear when the spirit, far from falling, turned around and rushed upon him." Despite this, the chase resumed.

Finally, the demon was corralled into a barn—but there it *vanished!* Not until a trap door was discovered was the mystery solved: the farmer had costumed himself in a complete bull's hide, which "had secured him from pistol shot" and accounted for the horns and tail. "The rogue confessed all his tricks," says Walpole, "and was pardoned on paying the arrears due for five years, at the old rent of the land." This was a popular tale, often being reprinted with no hint that it *might* be a product of Walpole's rich imagination.[25]

1804: Francis Smith investigated the Hammersmith Ghost case.

1823: Images of armed ghost hunters weren't confined to Britain. A short story titled "The Haunted Chamber," published in the U.S., features a traveler crossing Massachusetts when it was still a colony. He stops at an inn and learns it has a haunted chamber. The room had been long abandoned due to the visitations, though there was disagreement in what had been reported "concerning the nature of these nocturnal disturbances." The *only* agreement was that a spectral voice inquired, "Do you want to be shaved?" The ghost had been identified as a barber who was robbed and killed in that same room.

To debunk the haunting, the traveler proposes to spend the night there. The innkeeper accepts the plan. Once in the room, the traveler investigates it carefully. To strengthen his resolve, he begins talking to himself:

'Against human visitants, here is my protection,' said he, drawing forth a small case of pistols and placing them in the chair, 'and from superhuman ones, I have not much to fear.'

After some time in bed, the traveler grows confident that there is no ghost. That's when a disembodied voice asks, "Do you want to be shaved?" He pulls his pistols closer. He then hears a *scream*—and grabs his guns. Again, he is asked if he wants a shave! Another scream!

Only then does he solve the mystery: there's a tree branch close beside the inn, and "when the wind blew strongly in a particular direction, it caused friction against the glass of the window, producing a sharp grating sound." Imagination and expectation explained the rest. The tale ends with the traveler breaking off the branch and then teaching the locals a lesson by disguising himself as the ghost. Like a folktale, this story wound its way through the stateside press for decades.[26]

1825: In a letter to the editor of London's *Weekly Dispatch,* a writer identified as "S." shares an anecdote involving some of the year-round residents of Ramsgate, a seaside vacation spot. During the off-season, rumors of a ghost rose. "Accounts varied as to its size, shape, and appearance," says the writer. Nonetheless, "a party of men determined to lay at watch near the haunted spot." One carried a pistol, another a hefty club, yet another "one of Falstaff's pocket-pistols, *charged* with brandy." In other words, the men were armed and drinking.

At first, the outing was disappointing. The men were about ready to abandon their nocturnal surveillance, when suddenly "a white form was seen moving at a distance." S. says the men hailed it *three times,* but no reply was returned. Tension was high, and one of the men

> presented his pistol and gave fire. A loud scream followed the report, and a female rushed forward, wounded in the face and hand. Fortunately, our *ghost-hunters* had kept at such a respectful distance that the lady was not much hurt. . . .

S. ends the letter by asking the editor to "please caution all *valiant* gentlemen not to fire at a ghost till they are sure of their game."[27] Though the tale is told with a strain of dark humor, its moral might be considered a darkly serious one.

1842: In 1835, the residents of Joseph Procter's house—which stood beside a mill in Willington, England—started to experience strange noises and two apparitions. The manifestations had come and gone for five years when Edward Drury got permission to spend the night there. Though the family wasn't present, a mill employee was assigned to admit the ghost hunter. Drury recounted the investigation to Procter in letters, and one dated July 13, 1840, includes this passage: "I must here mention that, not expecting you at home, I had in my pocket a brace of pistols, determining in my mind to let one of them drop, as if by accident, before the miller, for fear he should presume to play tricks upon me." Drury assures Procter that the guns were not loaded, though. He then claims that, while looking at a closet, "I distinctly saw [the door] open and also saw the figure of a female attired in greyish garments. . . . It advanced with an apparently cautious step across the floor towards me." Drury rushed at the specter, but fell and remained "in an agony of fear and terror" for about three hours.[28] The paranormal investigator left as a believer in ghosts, and in this case, guns served only as a bluff to prevent pranks.

As the Victorian era progressed, the pendulum shifted back in the direction of believing in ghosts or, at least, keeping an open mind about them. Of course, many disbelievers continued to state their views, too, but paranormal investigators became more focused on *testing* ethereal possibilities than on *debunking* them. Ghost hunters holstered their weapons.

However, back in the early 1800s—back when Francis Smith killed Thomas Millwood—the assumption was that ghosts can bleed. This explains why Smith and those other ghost hunters on Black Lion Lane were armed.

It's not quite enough to explain why Smith pulled the trigger, though.

Ghosts Are Difficult to Bury

"I don't believe in them, but I fear them."

So said Germaine de Staël (1766-1817) when discussing ghosts—that is, according to an 1872 memoir by Henry Holland. De Staël was a prominent figure in French letters and politics, and assuming Holland remembered things correctly a half century after her death, she had offered a quick but smart insight into how an individual—or a whole society—can be of two minds about spectral phenomena. The logical part of one's brain says "no, ghosts aren't real" while the emotional self says "and *yet—!*" It's a contradiction that's also a keen insight into human nature, one that echoes Samuel Johnson's comment on the same subject: "All argument is against it; but all belief is for it."[29]

De Staël wasn't alone in stopping short of *completely* rejecting the reality of ghosts. As far back as 1725, historian and founding folklorist Henry Bourne said that people, especially those raised with fireside ghost stories, might *think* they've seen real phantoms, but it can be traced to fear-induced imagination or hearsay. Then comes an important qualifier:

> Not that there have not been or may not be apparitions. We know that there have undoubtedly been such things and that there still are upon particular occasions. But almost all the stories of ghosts and spirits are grounded on no other bottom than the fears and fancies and weak brains of men."[30]

Bourne is urging readers to scoot toward the skeptical side of the sliding scale of believing in ghosts—but to avoid reaching its extreme end.

We see traces of the same thing during the campaign against ghosts, when taking an extreme position had become fairly common. Introducing that collection of ghost stories that, like Radcliffe's novels, end with *natural* explanations, Taylor admits he personally leaves some room for the possibility of ghosts:

> I would by no means wish it to be imagined that I am sceptical in my opinions or entirely disbelieve and set my face against all apparitional record. No, I do believe that, for certain purposes and on certain and all-wise occasions, such things *are* and *have been* permitted by the Almighty.[31]

This is the "nothing is impossible with God" argument that Bigland refutes. At the same time, Taylor is suggesting one can go too far in dismissing supernatural visitations.

By 1830, readers got an update of sorts on how well the campaign against ghosts was going. Identified only as Anslem, the writer says:

> The belief in ghosts and hobgoblins, in fact, is the basis and keystone of all superstition, and though 'the march

of intellect' has of late years done away a good deal with the prejudices of the 'times of old,' yet it still lurks and probably will ever continue to do so. . . ."

After a summary of supernatural beliefs lingering in Scotland, Germany, and Italy, readers are then treated to a retelling of a ghost story Anslem once heard from a friend. This friend had attended Oxford University, where he and a fellow student fell in love with the same woman. A duel ensued, and the friend killed his rival with a sword. Duels were illegal, however, so he fled England. As they tend to do, the ghost of the killed man caught up with him. This apparition was enough to prompt the friend to return home, where it turned out he was acquitted of the crime and never again saw the ghost. This narrative comes from "a man of the strictest veracity and honour," says Anslem, who feels "bound to believe that which in other circumstances I should certainly have been slow to give credence to." Indeed, before relating similar eyewitness stories, Anslem explains, "I hold it wisest to steer a middle course" in regard to the reliability of those narratives.[32] Here's an example of someone who—after decades of influential voices rallying to bury ghosts once and for all—is still open to the possibility that they walk among us.

Was Smith similarly open to this possibility? As he shivered on a dark street that January night, was there still some small part of him wondering if he might encounter an *actual* ghost? This would explain why, upon barely making out a figure—a dimly *white* figure—he twice demanded, "Who are you, and what are you?" It would be strange if his including *"what* are you" were an inquiry about the figure's profession or status as a hoaxer. It was more likely directed at the figure being something living or dead. And, when that *who* or that *what* remained mute, panic might have burst loose. Perhaps Smith's muscles contracted, including those in his trigger finger.

CERTAIN NOCTURNAL DISTURBANCES

Millwood's silence can be explained by his being *more thoroughly* convinced that believing in ghosts was absurd. Did the headstrong 22-year-old stay silent because he was convinced Smith's question was too ridiculous to deserve an answer? Previously, he had threatened to punch a man for suggesting he was a ghost. His failure to reply here might have risen from a refusal to dignify such a question with an answer or possibly even from an effort to restrain himself when presented with such ignorance.

Possibly.

These speculations find their foundation when we place the Hammersmith tragedy in social context. There were widespread pressures to move British society into a new era, a new century of "enlightenment." Antiquated prejudices would be eradicated, and so would deeply ingrained beliefs that reached back for millennia. Instead of promoting open-minded acceptance of differing perspectives, the goal was to attain conformity and consensus by labeling those who believed in ghosts as "superstitious" and "ignorant." This only exacerbated the differences and stirred confusion. History is filled with examples of conflict and bloodshed arising—not just from differing convictions—but from well-intended yet arrogant efforts to convert one group to another's views.

On January 3, 1804, the history of ghost hunting came to reflect this pattern.

---

[1] In this era, newspapers and magazines routinely copied articles from each other. One reprinted piece contains this sentence about Thomas Millwood: "The ill-fated man was dressed as usual in his white flannel jacket, and, having parted with his sister at his own door, proceeded along Black Lion Lane, where the ghost-hunters were lying in wait." It's in "Melancholy Accident," *True Briton*, January 6, 1804, p. 4; "Singular Accident," *Lincoln, Rutland, and Stamford Mercury,* January 13, 1804, p.1; "Affairs in England," *Scots Magazine* 66 (January

1804) p. 68; and "Domestic Incidents," *Universal Magazine* 1 (January 1804) p. 63.

² "Melancholy Catastrophe," *St. James's Chronicle,* January 5, 1804, p. 4. "The Real Hammersmith Ghost," *St. James's Chronicle,* January 10, 1804, p. 2. "Coroner's Inquests," *Star,* January 6, 1804, p. 4.

³ "The Hammersmith Ghost," *Star,* January 9, 1804, p. 3. "The Real Hammersmith Ghost," p. 2. *Newgate Calendar,* edited by George Theodore Wilkinson, vol. 3 (Printed for Thomas Kelly, 1814) p. 122. *The Newgate Calendar,* edited by Andrew Knapp and William Baldwin, vol. 3 (J. Robins and Co., 1825) p. 361.

⁴ "The Hammersmith Ghost, p. 3.

⁵ *Old Bailey Proceedings Online, 1674-1913* (www. oldbaileyonline.org, version 8.0, March 2018) January 1804, trial of Francis Smith (t18040111-79). Citations below refer to this source as *"OBP."* "Coroner's Inquests," p. 4.

⁶ The reward was mentioned by John Locke at the coroner's inquest. The *Star* reported: "He had never heard of any formal reward having been offered for apprehending the Ghost, but he believed a clergyman and another gentleman had promised to give five guineas each to whoever should discover who it was." "Coroner's Inquests," p. 4. At Smith's trial, Locke confirmed that the night Millwood died was especially dark and that Black Lion Lane was bordered by hedges, making it dark on any night. He elaborated, "[I]f it was a light night, it would be dark in the lane. Though it is not wider than from me to you, (about four yards,) you could not perceive anybody on the other side of it." *OBP,* January 1804, Francis Smith (t18040111-79). This explains why Black Lion Lane was "one of the places by which the ghost used to make its escape when hard pressed by its pursuers," as noted in "Melancholy Catastophe," p. 4.

⁷ *OBP,* January 1804, Francis Smith (t18040111-79).

⁸ That Thomas's wife was "at a short distance at work" is found in Ann's testimony at the inquest. See "Coroner's Inquests," p. 4. At the trial, she specified that her sister-in-law "was at Mr. Smith's, the Out-riders." See *OBP,* January 1804, Francis Smith (t18040111-79). The rest of her account comes from the latter source.

⁹ Smith's emotional state, the events following the shooting, and Smith's compliant apprehension are found in *OBP,* January 1804, Francis Smith (t18040111-79). Millwood's fatal injury is detailed in "Coroner's Inquests," p. 4.

[10] "London," *St. James's Chronicle*, January 24-26, 1804, p. 1. That Smith only served one year in prison is confirmed by George Courtney Lyttleton in *The Modern History of England, Continued from the Commencement of Hostilities in the Year 1903* (J. Stratford, 1804) p. 484.

[11] *The Sun*, January 9, 1804, p. 3.

[12] *OBP*, January 1804, Francis Smith (t18040111-79).

[13] *OBP*, January 1804, Francis Smith (t18040111-79). "Murder—Hammersmith Ghost," *St. James's Chronicle*, January 14, 1804, p. 3. In a way, Fulbrooke was giving Smith's defense team what they wanted by suggesting that the shooting was an understandable mistake. Ann Millwood was asked if she had expressed concerns to her brother, given his workclothes matching the guise of the "ghost." She negated the possibility that Thomas was guilty of wrongdoing *and* says she didn't caution him about others making that mistake.

[14] "Coroner's Inquests," p. 4.

[15] John Alderson, "On Apparitions," *Edinburgh Medical and Surgical Journal* 6 (July 1810) pp. 287-96. John Alderson, *An Essay on Apparitions, in which Their Appearance Is Accounted for by Causes Wholly Independent of Preternatural Agency* (Longman, et al., 1823). For other physicians exploring similar territory, see John Ferriar, *An Essay towards a Theory of Apparitions* (Printed for Cadell and Davies by J. and J. Haddock, 1813) and Samuel Hibbert, *Sketches of the Philosophy of Apparitions; or, An Attempt to Trace Such Illusions to Their Physical Causes* (Oliver & Boyd, 1825).

[16] Owen Davies, *The Haunted: A Social History of Ghosts* (Palgrave Macmillan, 2007) pp. 187, 193-194.

[17] "Phantasmagoria; The Manner of Raising Ghosts and Spectres," *Caledonian Mercury*, March 25, 1802, p. 1.

[18] Joseph Taylor, *Apparitions; or, The Mystery of Ghosts, Hobgoblins, and Haunted Houses Developed* (Lackington, Allen, Co., 1814) pp. vi, xi, 13.

[19] William Shenstone," An Opinion of Ghosts," *The Works, in Verse and Prose, of William Shenstone, Esq.*, vol. 2 (Printed for R. and J. Dodsley, 1764) pp. 68-74.

[20] John Bigland, "Essays XXII-XIV," *Essays on Various Subjects*, vol. 1 (Printed by and for W. Sheardown, 1805) pp. 158, 165-166, 179, 182, 195.

[21] John Anderson, *The Young Woman's Guide to Virtue, Economy, and Happiness* (Printed by Mackenzie and Dent, 1817) pp. 424-425.

[22] I quote from a reprint, one which identifies the author as "a country clergyman," *The Death-Watch: Dialogues upon Spirits* (Printed for W. Baynes, 1796) pp. 25, 63. This is confirmed to be Weightman's book with a new title by Jonathan Barry in "News from the Invisible World: The Publishing History of Tales of the Supernatural c. 1660-1832, *Cultures of Witchcraft in Europe from the Middle Ages to the Present,* edited by Jonathan Barry, Owen Davies, and Cornelie Usborne (Palgrave Macmillan, 2018) p. 207. Frances Maria MacDonald, "Sermon XXII," *Twenty-Four Sermons, Calculated for Sermons,* vol. 2 (Printed by the Philanthropic Society, 1819) p. 97.

[23] Peter Henry Bruce, *Memoirs of Peter Henry Bruce, Esq., A Military Officer in the Services of Prussia, Russia, and Great Britain* (Printed for the Author's Widow and Sold by T. Payne and Son, 1782) pp. 304-306

[24] Elizabeth Gunning, *The Packet,* vol. 4 (Printed for J. Bell, 1794) p. 5.

[25] Horace Walpole, "CLXXXII: Real Apparition," *Walpoliana,* vol. 2 (Printed for R. Phillips, 1799) pp. 131-136. The anecdote's lasting appeal is seen in its being reprinted—without mentioning Walpole—as "The Interested Apparition," *Lady's Monthly Museum* 16 (March 1806) pp. 175-177; "A Real Ghost—No Joke!!!," *The Casket* 1 (September 15, 1827) pp. 257-258; and "A French Ghost Story," *Alden's Oxford Monthly* 2 (February 1872) p. 230. Evidence that Walpole had a rich imagination is found in his having authored *A Castle of Otrantro* (1764), which is generally said to have ignited the popularity of Gothic novels in the late 1700s.

[26] "The Haunted Chamber," *The Waste Book,* vol. 1 (Printed by John Miller, 1823) pp. 23-32. A decade later, the tale was retold, with the same title in *The Literary Journal* 1 (September 21, 1833) p. 124. Both of those were published in Rhode Island, but a decade afterward, the traveler had gone west: "The Barber's Ghost," *Salt River Journal* [Bowling Green, Missouri], January 30, 1841, p. 1. This new title was reused a couple of decades later, when our man returned to his home state in Boston's *Gleason's Literary Companion* 5 (July 2, 1864) p. 432. Still restless, he reappeared in the South two-and-a-half decades later: "The Barber's Ghost," *Yorkville Enquirer* [South Carolina], July 31, 1889, p. 4.

[27] "Rural Sports—Ghost-Shooting," *Weekly Dispatch* [London], December 4, 1825, p. 6.

---

[28] "Authentic Account of a Visit to the Haunted House at Willington," *The Local Historian's Table Book,* edited by M.A. Richardson, vol. 1 (M.A. Richardson, 1842) p. 303.

[29] Henry Holland, *Recollections of Past Life* (Longmans, Green and Co., 1872) p. 113. Johnson is quoted in James Boswell, *The Life of Samuel Johnson, LL.D.* vol. 2 (Printed by Henry Baldwin, 1791) p. 190.

[30] Henry Bourne, *Antiquitates Vulgares; or, The Antiquities of the Common People* (Printed by J. White, 1725) pp. 76-77.

[31] Taylor, p. vii.

[32] Anslem, "A Chapter on Ghosts," *Pocket Magazine* 2 (July 1830) pp. 29-33. Anslem, "Another Chapter on Ghosts," *Pocket Magazine* 2 (August 1830) p. 132.

CHAPTER EIGHT

PREACHING PATIENCE: CHARLES CALEB COLTON AND THE SAMPFORD MYSTERY

The Chave residence was in the village of Sampford Peverell, Devonshire, England. Around 1810, ghostly phenomena occurred there that were fairly routine in some ways. The apparition of a woman was reported. There were disembodied footsteps. Knocking was heard, and if one knocked first, the pattern was repeated. In other ways, the manifestations were distinctive. They sometimes occurred during the day. A candlestick, a bible, and a sword were tossed by invisible hands. Bed curtains didn't just waft— they *shook* on their own. Whatever was invading the house could also be dangerous because those who slept in a particular room were beaten, and they left the room with bumps, bruises, and numbness.

There were several investigators. However, one man stood out as the primary ghost hunter and chronicler of the haunting. That man was the Reverend Charles Caleb Colton, and by his own account, he approached the case with a resolutely open mind. He was neither intent on debunking the case nor interested in confirming it to be a supernatural event. He simply wanted to get at the truth. He even offered financial incentive to anyone who could give an adequate explanation. But no one came to collect it.

The case baffled those living when it happened as well as in the decades to follow. An 1813 source says, "With respect to the ghost, we confess we know not what to make of it" and "the narrative is altogether unaccountable." As suggested by his title, the author of the 1837 book *Sketches of Imposture, Deception, and Credulity* clearly suspects *someone* perpetrated a hoax—but "the mischievous disturber of Sampford Peverell remains to this day undiscovered." The puzzle persisted well into the Victorian era. In 1883, for instance, a biographer of Colton says, "The mystery was never wholly solved; but mysteries made up of conspiracy on the one side and credulity on the other, or of fact and supposition in equal proportions, are not perhaps susceptible of very complete explanation." The very next year, in a book about Britain's many, many haunted houses, the writer addresses this case:

> Again and again has it been asserted that the whole matter has been found out, the fraud has been discovered, the perpetrators have confessed, and so forth; and yet, as in so many other cases, when these allegations have been investigated they have been found to be baseless, and the mystery remains as much a mystery as ever.[1]

The Cock Lane Ghost had been debunked. Few at all took the Hammersmith Ghost to be anything more than some creep in a sheet. However, despite various efforts to explain the Sampford Ghost, the case file remains open.

Colton ensured that the file stay open by rejecting easy theories about fakery that didn't account for all the facts. In this regard, he served as a model for ghost hunters to come, a founder of the attitude toward paranormal investigation that crystalized in the Victorian era. He personally postponed making decisions and publicly encouraged others do the same.

Before exploring that, here's the case as chronicled by the newspapers—in particularly, by a journalist named John William Marriott—and by Colton himself.

On August 2, 1810, London's *Morning Chronicle* printed a letter to the editor, one dated the day before. The writer, identified only as J.D., wished to share a "well-authenticated" tale about the residents of a Devonshire farmhouse. They had been "very much disturbed and alarmed by noises, which human reason is incapable to account for." Respected members of the community investigated. Assuming it was a hoax, the neighbors questioned the family. The responses were convincing enough that some gentlemen conducted nocturnal surveillance and were "fully satisfied that the singular noises there heard are supernatural."

J.D. says the sounds primarily emanated from one room, which I'll refer to as Case's room, since a young maid named Sally Case usually slept there. However, the phantom also made itself known in other areas of the house. Noises appeared in another bedroom, too, one occupied by a different servant. In that same spot, "an old sword that hangs behind the bed is violently shook, and something is heard to pace the room." Even more unsettling, the ghost lays on the bed—and on whoever happens to be in it. This invisible weight is so heavy, a child sharing the bed "nearly suffocated" beneath it! The ghost had also visited the homeowner's bedroom, where it spun a candlestick "with the greatest velocity." Elsewhere identified as Chave, the man "attempted to ring his bell, when the candlestick was thrown with great violence at the bed's head, but fortunately missed the farmer." No explanation was found in a search that immediately followed.[2] Exactly what inspired J.D. to share this story is not mentioned. Let's assume it simply felt newsworthy.

Indeed, other London newspapers pounced on the story, reprinting the information in the letter within a matter of days and even *hours!* The village of Sampford Peverell was receiving more attention than usual, and it wasn't the kind of attention some residents liked. Marriott made it clear that such superstitious nonsense would be debunked in the newspaper he edited, the *Taunton Courier,* which served a wide readership in England's West Country. On August 16, the once-a-week paper not only used the term "the Sampford Ghost," but also announced that it would respond to the London press. Specifically, Marriott declared that "the claims of this *dark visitor,* shall, in our next [issue], be set forth in a *proper light* to the public."[3] *Before* launching an investigation into the matter, he made his position clear: Marriott was intent on ending this travesty.

Curiously, in that next week's issue, Marriott says he will postpone his response for another week, assuring his readers that he would "then be able to completely satisfy the public" by revealing that the startling events at the Chave house "have their origin in disgusting imposture and villainous delusion." The reason for the delay, he explains, is to make space for a report from someone who had already looked into the haunting, someone who says he went to the site with no preconceived ideas of what he'd find.

That man was Colton. His letter opens by saying: "It is not the object of this letter to make converts to a belief in ghosts. . . ." He goes on to explain that he wouldn't have written at all

> had not many stories already got into circulation, so
> very contradictory, that the credibility of facts which
> certainly have taken place, is utterly destroyed by
> the palpable absurdity of other stories so ridiculous

that they carry their own confutation of them.

This is another way of saying he wanted to cut through the misinformation and set the record straight.

Much of what Colton says makes him appear to be an astute and thorough ghost hunter. He spent six nights, not all in a row, at the Chave residence. There, he conducted "the most minute investigation and closest inspection of the premises." To catch a hoaxer, he even tried sealing "every door, cavity, etc. in the house" with paper, but these seals remained unbroken even though "the phenomena that night were as unaccountable as ever." He questioned witnesses who lived at the house, finding them to be genuinely unable to account for the phenomena. He met with visitors who had slept in the house, all of them reporting that "their night's rest was invariably destroyed by violent blows from some invisible hand," opening and closing of the bed curtains, a "suffocating and almost inexpressible weight," and by noises "so loud at times to shake the whole room." In all, he spoke with "more than twenty people of credibility, quite unconnected with the owner," who claimed to have had bizarre experiences at the Chave house—and, if asked, they would each take an oath to support their claims.

Despite having conducted a solid examination of the situation, Colton refrains from taking a stance on exactly what is happening. He declares himself

utterly unable to account for any of the phenomena I have there seen and heard, and labour at this moment under no small perplexity, arising from a determination not lightly to admit of supernatural interference, and an impossibility of hitherto tracing these effects to any human cause.

While hesitant to proclaim the house to be haunted by actual ghosts, Colton found nothing more concrete to explain what was happening there. In essence, he decided the case was *as-yet-undecided.*

To reinforce this position, the clergyman declares that he was ready to "forfeit a very considerable sum to the poor of my parish" if the phenomena were found "to have been produced by any human art or ingenuity." It's not a reward exactly, but it's an incentive that might prompt a citizen who's more noble than self-interested. After making this gesture, he provides the names of seven men—from lawyer and surgeon to merchant and innkeeper—who "are ready, if called on, to depose to their having witnessed circumstances in this house at Sampford, to them perfectly inexplicable and for which they are utterly unable to account." Even Colton's own account is presented as certified by the local Master of Chancery, giving it the weight of an affidavit.[4] Already, readers of the *Taunton Courier* were presented with a contrast between Colton—unbiased, methodical, and patient— and Marriott, who said he was itching to defraud the haunting but who also seemed to be stalling in actually doing so.

Like Samuel Johnson half a century earlier, Colton's interest in the case branded him a gullible dupe. London's *Examiner* dubbed him the "Reverend Believer." After reprinting excerpts of the letter, the editorialist ridicules Colton for his offer to donate to the poor in exchange for information: "It will not be a little amusing, to see for once ignorance and super-stition productive of charitable results, and what Mr. Colton even loses in money he will gain in commonsense, an article with which he appears to be not overburthened." Marriott's promise to expose the fraud is dealt with warmly: "we heartily wish the Editor success in his ghostly labours." It might come as no surprise that the editors of the *Examiner,* brothers John and Leigh Hunt, had been professional associates of Marriott before the latter moved west to start his own paper.[5] The situation was turning into a war of words between a country vicar and a fraternity of journalists.

Marriot's attempt to debunk the haunting finally arrived the following week—or, rather, its *first step* was taken in the August 30 issue of the *Taunton Courier.* This initial article ends with the teaser for "many other particulars in this vile farce" in the following week's issue. However, that *second* installment was postponed *another* week because Marriott had heard from someone claiming to provide "the most indisputable evidence of the very gross deception that has been practiced." At last, in a two-part article published on September 13 and 20, readers were informed of a well-orchestrated plot lurking at the Chave residence.

Across these articles, Marriott makes a series of allegations, many of which seem designed to paint the haunting as either ridiculous or highly suspicious. I've altered the order of their original presentation, but these claims include:

#1) A former resident of the house earned a good living by selling smuggled contraband.

#2) When that resident died, a Mr. Talley inherited the house and lived there for two years.

#3) Talley then rented it to Chave. The house needed repairs, and Talley agreed to pay for them. However, upon receiving a bill from a painter hired by Chave without Talley's approval, tensions rose between the landlord and tenant. Chave assumed he was going to be thrown out of the house.

#4) Only then did the *alleged* spectral visitations

occur. No disturbances had ever been reported at the house prior to the Chaves moving in, and they had only been there seven months.

Marriott later portrayed these reports as absurd by comparing them to long-outdated beliefs in witchcraft:

> The vassals of witchcraft awoke from their slumbers—the Prince of Darkness held his Court at Sampford—thousands assembled to pay him homage, and the tail of his Satanic Majesty became dignified with a tassel of very imposing effect, in the affidavit of the Rev. C. Colton.

#5) Two investigators went to the house, hoping to spend the night. They were denied. The next morning, they met with Chave and learned that the "monster" looked like "a black rabbit, only wonderfully larger." The men were allowed into Case's room, where they stomped in the hope that the spectral stomping would be returned. Nothing happened. In an adjacent room, the men found floorboards removed, leaving a gap of "considerable hollow depth." The implication is that one could make noises in Case's room through that gap.

#6) Talley insisted upon spending the night at the house. Presumably, he wanted to expose a scheme to make the property undesirable, which would increase the chances of Chave remaining as a tenant and possibly allow him to purchase the house at a low price. Upon arrival, Talley spotted Mrs. Chave conferring with a local man named Dodge, who promised to return and quickly left. However, when the landlord crossed a room leading to Case's, where he intended to spend the night, he found Dodge concealed behind a bed curtain. He also found a mop nearby, with which he concluded the loud noises could be made by banging the ceiling on the floor below. The next morning, he found support for his hunch in tattered marks on the end of the mopstick and on the ceiling directly below Case's room.

#7) Talley also found a well-used bludgeon hidden in the chimney in Case's room.

#8) Mrs. Chave's brother, Taylor—who occupied the room beside Case's—had trained under a man named Moon, who was a successful sleight-of-hand and conjuring performer. Taylor had convinced Case to join him in faking the haunting.

#9) The slaps Case received—and which Colton said he had heard in the dark—were self-inflicted. This explains why she continued to sleep in the room.

#10) The house was constructed with supports, called "battens," allowing the resonances needed to make the "ghost" seem to roam from room to room.

Toward the end of the last article, Marriott replaces "Sampford Ghost" with "Sampford Conspiracy" and scolds Colton for his ongoing efforts "in sanctioning an infamous imposture and in maintaining an opinion so unworthy a clergyman." The publisher concludes with a willingness to "engage to prove the foregoing statement in any Court of Judicature in the Kingdom."[6] Yet he offers no sources anywhere in the articles. For instance, did Talley provide him with information? Neither does Marriott offer any means to verify the claims. If someone wanted to, say, confirm that Taylor had been a student of Moon, how could that be done? Marriott weaves together a fascinating theory, but its threads are easily snapped.

In fact, Colton quickly went to work at unraveling Marriott's conspiracy theory. At some point—knowing that newspapers could not afford him the space he needed—he penned a pamphlet titled *Sampford Ghost:*

A Plain and Authentic Narrative. He opens by reiterating his inability to explain the phenomena at the Chave house without more data. "It is by no means my intention," he says, "to attempt to prove in these pages or disprove the existence of ghosts, neither do I have any opinion on this subject." Following a reprint of the letter he had sent to the *Taunton Courier* and a response to the bashing he received from the *Examiner,* Colton introduces several details gathered during his investigation. As if with Marriott's theory in mind, he says he will relate only facts that "are well known in this neighborhood to have taken place, and which can, if required, be substantiated on the oaths of credible and reliable witnesses."[7] Of course, this claim about the reliability of his facts might be false itself—but at least Colton is mindful of how he presents his case.

Scattered throughout all of his new details, Colton contradicts claims made by Marriott. For instance, though the house's unexplained disturbances "became extremely troublesome" four months earlier, "long before that time, some very unaccountable things had occasionally taken place in it." More than once, a boy had reported an "apparition of a woman" and heard "extraordinary sounds at night." It's hard to say exactly how this jives with Marriott's contention that the alleged paranormal activity started only after tensions rose between Chave and Talley (as claimed in #3 and #4 above), but it casts a shadow over the Marriot's timeline.

Colton also acknowledges the loose floorboards over the gap in the room leading to Case's (#5), saying it was probably a hiding place left by the previous occupants/smugglers (#1). He "always most narrowly watched" this cavity, covering it or even booby-trapping it to ensure that it played no part in creating the phenomena. Similarly, the chimney in Case's room "has been regularly examined," putting Talley's discovery of a bludgeon there (#7) into some doubt.

According to Marriott, the battens used to carry sound throughout the house (#10) are common knowledge to "any mason's apprentice, however stupid." He mocks Colton's education for his failure to catch how that trick was produced. In contrast, Colton suggests that, if it *were* a trick, he was far from alone in being fooled. He explains that the knockings would appear at mid-day, "above stairs or below," and "any person or persons (for at times more than a dozen witnesses have been present at once) on ascending the stairs and stamping loudly with their feet, would be answered somewhat louder." The sounds even followed people around and could shift rapidly from one spot to another.[8] This effect might have been created with the mopstick (#6), but resonating battens don't explain how such focus could be achieved. And readers could reasonably wonder how not even one of those "more than a dozen witnesses" grew suspicious enough to catch someone banging a stick on the ceiling below.

Colton does not aim his *Plain and Authentic Narrative* directly at the *Taunton Chronicle* articles. However, once Marriott reprinted his own articles in pamphlet form,[9] the clergyman had more to say. He said it very directly—and with a sharp edge—in yet another pamphlet, this one titled *Sampford Ghost: Stubborn Facts Against Vague Assertions.* Here, Colton refutes virtually every one of Marriott's claims point by point.

There are too many of these direct refutations for me to review here, but I will give a few good examples. Marriot's claims that Talley lived at the house two years (#2) before the Chaves had occupied it for seven months (#4) don't accord with the records of the local excise man, which put Talley's time there as significantly shorter and the Chaves' as significantly longer. The tensions that supposedly rose between Talley and Chave over the painter's bill (#3) were actually between Talley and the *painter*. Similarly, the tattered mopstick, the resonating battens, and the ceiling dents, are all addressed and dismissed.

Dodge, Taylor, and Case—the main players in Marriott's alleged conspiracy—are each proven innocent. It's true that Mrs. Chave and Dodge had a conversation on the night of Talley's investigation (#6), but it was to arrange for Dodge to sleep beside "an apprenticed boy who had been frightened by something in the house." That's why Talley found Dodge in the room leading to Case's. The latter couldn't have been hiding behind a bed curtain, "for the plainest of all possible reasons: THERE WERE NO CURTAINS to that bed on which he saw Dodge sitting." Colton points out that even Talley himself now admits this.

The allegation that Taylor studied under the stage magician Moon (#8) is also examined. Colton writes:

The public would be much obliged to Mr. Marriott if he would inform them the time and the place, the when and the where, Mr. Taylor received this marvellous education under Mr. Moon. Mr. Moon himself does not remember one iota of the circumstance. Mr. Taylor and all his relations are ready to swear to the utter falsehood of the whole assertion.

The notion that Taylor coerced Case into beating herself in the dark (#9) is cast in doubt when Colton names another victim who, like Case, was beaten and claimed to see "a large arm suspended over the bed without any body attached to it." In addition, Colton includes a sworn statement from Dodge, Taylor, and Case to affirm that "they are entirely ignorant of the cause of all those extraordinary circumstances that have and are occurring at the house of Mr. Chave in the parish of Sampford."[10] Isn't that exactly what they would swear if they were guilty? Maybe so, but if the trio were to be caught, this would add perjury to their criminal offences.

At the end of this second pamphlet, Colton reaffirms his decision to remain undecided until far better evidence is found. "Time may do much for us in developing this mystery," he writes, adding that, "while it continues, there is a chance of discovering it, and it has by no means ceased." (Here, *discovering* it means uncovering its secrets.) Two years later, he made a similar comment. Even then, "the slightest shadow of an explanation has not yet been given" for the strange phenomena, and "it is well known to all in this neighborhood that they continue with unabated violence to this hour."[11] In other words, what might best be called the Sampford *Mystery* continued—not just its weird displays, but its lack of an explanation for them, too.

The Sampford case is remembered more for the skirmish between Colton and Marriott than for anything especially unique about the ghostly manifestations or about a hoax being unveiled. Perhaps Marriott was very deliberately creating a sensational tale—and stringing his readers along—only to sell newspapers. Perhaps Colton *was* being duped by charlatans or, as we'll see some have contended, a collaborator with and spokesperson for those charlatans.

However, what makes the case significant in terms of ghost hunting is *not* in knowing which man was right or wrong. Instead, it's in their very different approaches to dealing with the mystery. What truly matters here is the wait-and-see strategy advocated by Colton. By steadfastly championing patience, he became a harbinger of—and possibly model for—the coming generations of ghost hunters of the Victorian period.

Aching for An Answer

While the Sampford Ghost case was *generally* interpreted to be unsolved and remembered that way decades afterward, some commentators looking back on it choose to settle the matter. Unfortunately, they disagree on an explanation. A quick review of these clashing conclusions will illustrate how the urge to resolve a mystery is strong enough in some people that insufficient evidence doesn't stand in the way.

At least one commentator holds that Colton was a key figure in the conspiracy. This view is purported in an 1892 history of Tiverton, a town near Sampford. Turning to the Chave haunting, Frederick John Snell says:

> The affair will always be wrapt in a certain amount of mystery, although the prevailing belief was, and still is, that it was the result of some conspiracy; and suspicion points to the Rev. Mr. Colton, who certainly took a great interest in the matter, as the arch conspirator.[12]

Snell offers nothing to support this. I suppose, if one worked hard enough, one might appreciate the flake of flattery in being dubbed an *arch* conspirator in an event that one had written about to promote patience, truth, and ethical journalism.

In another regional history, this one devoted to all of Devonshire and published in 1908, S. Baring-Gould addresses the century-old case. After declaring that "Mr. Marriott was doubtless right in his conjecture that there was a plot among the servants," he adds:

> There can, I think, be little doubt that it was not Mr.
> Chave, but the maid-servants who managed the whole
> series of phenomena. These knockings could easily be
> transmitted through boards, and the curtains tossed
> about, and books and candlesticks flung across the
> room, by having horsehairs attached to them. That is the
> true secret of the Poltergeist manifestations in England,
> France, and Germany.

It's possible Baring-Gould was mixing the Sampford Ghost
with an exposed hoax in Stockwell, which "became almost
as celebrated in the annals of superstition as Cock Lane,"
according to a book about such deceptions. In 1772, a
servant named Anne Robinson periodically scared away her
elderly employer, thereby allowing herself the freedom to
entertain a lover. She first placed kitchen items on the brinks
of shelves and "attached horsehairs to other articles" to
create poltergeist-like effects with a discreet bump or an
inconspicuous tug.[13] While the servants in Sampford might
have had plenty of *opportunity* to fool the many who
investigated the Chave house, Baring-Gould never clarifies
what their *motive* was to do so.

Speaking of poltergeists, one of these invisible, non-
human entities that throw things, make a racket, and
sometimes even start fires is another contender in the short
parade of possibilities. In 1907, Charles W. Harper shared
his collection of historical ghost stories, retelling them with
affection for this narrative tradition and with a sense of
humor. Turning to the Chave haunting, he says, "It was
doubtless a poltergeist of unusual endurance, or a company
of poltergeists who relieved one another in the work, who
originated and continued for more than three years the
infernal shindies at Sampford Peverell." Though readers
aren't meant to take Harper entirely seriously, the mani-

festations actually *do* follow the general pattern of polter-geist phenomena, making this a rare paranormal explanation.

Nevertheless, charges of fakery dominate this haunting, and Harper next turns to a more natural explanation. He includes an interesting update from the Reverend Philip C. Rossiter, a Sampford resident since 1874. Rossiter reports that the current resident of the house said some of the walls were "double, with a passage in between," allowing a hoaxer to come and go pretty easily. This leads Rossiter to theorize that "the noises were caused by smugglers." He once had known "a very old smuggler" who told him that, if pursued by officials, his colleagues would sneak their contraband inland. On occasion, they would go "as far as Sampford Peverell." If the Chave house were being used as a warehouse for illegal goods, the smugglers "would wish to frighten the people to account for their noise in storing them."[14] The double walls harken back to the gap in the floor mentioned by Marriot and Colton, but both of them suggested there was only room enough to hide contraband or to waggle a mopstick. They both also mention that the house was reputed to have belonged to smugglers prior to Talley inheriting it. Still, if criminal operations had been continuing while the Chaves were there, how could investigators—especially Talley himself—have failed to foil it? With this question in mind, let's go ahead and add *smugglers* to the List of Maybes.

The urge to pin down a final answer without knowing *all* the facts or being able to account for them *logically*—that's what Colton wanted to curb. Theorizing and consid-ering possibilities have their place, but this should come only after extensive data gathering. Marriott presented his theory as if it were the truth, and that's a mistake Colton refused to make. Among the characteristics that would come to dominate ghost hunting in the Victorian era, securing abundant evidence before drawing conclusions stands out. This, then, is Colton's legacy to paranormal investigators.

The Victorians Gather Evidence

In 1839, two years after Victoria took the throne, a remarkable essay appeared in the *Cambridge University Magazine*. The journal is described as "a vehicle through which the Undergraduates, particularly of this university, may express their opinions."[15] The essay's title is "A Chapter on Ghosts," and the author is identified only with the Greek word for spirit or soul: ΨΥΧΗ. First, acknowledgement is made that the ideas to be presented will be met with resistance, given "these days of universal incredulity and sceptisim." Next comes assurance that the writer is someone who "has taken much pains to investigate the subject of apparitions, and whose fortune it has been to converse with several parties of the highest respectability and intelligence, whose most solemn assurances he cannot and will not distrust." Readers, it appears, are about to be asked to rethink their dismissal of the reality of ghosts.

Those readers quickly come to see that ΨΥΧΗ is well versed in logic. We're given a lesson about how a conviction based on *probability* can be weakened by contrary evidence—but a conviction founded on *proof* cannot be. "And this is the reason why 'a good ghost story' will generally stagger (or at least *interest,* which is much the same) the most incredulous, even though he be unwilling to admit that it does so," says the writer. He states that not believing in ghosts is grounded on a *probability* because we have no definitive *proof* for or against such belief.

Even scripture offers no proof. ΨΥΧΗ cites the passages about the apparition of Samuel appearing to Saul and the Witch of Endor as well as those about the bodies of many buried saints rising and appearing to the living alongside Christ's resurrection. While these might be "absolute miracles—that is, the only instances in which the course of nature was so interrupted," they remain more pro- than anti-ghost. Just the same, the writer says he'll look elsewhere to make his argument.

ΨYXH next carefully and cleverly examines two key propositions. They are:

1) That there is no positive evidence or proof whatever, nor even any very strong probability, against the reality of supernatural appearances.

2) That there is the strongest proof, amounting to moral certainty at least, *i.e.,* incontrovertible human testimony, in favour of the reality of such appearances.

I won't go into the specifics of how the writer supports these propositions and counterargues opposition to them, but here are samples of his intriguing points. The argument that ghostly visitations are "contrary to the usual laws of nature" is false because, if they appear, "their appearance is *not* absolutely *contrary to nature.*" While some hauntings are revealed to be hoaxes, it's not logical to assume *all* can be debunked—in fact, despite cooperation between university philosophers and London officers, a recent case near Cambridge's campus was never solved. Witness testimony, which is "always admitted as sufficient in other matters," should not be automatically disbelieved in regard to encounters with ghosts.[16] I'm especially struck by this last point, given the decisive role that witness testimony is given in so many jurisprudence systems across the globe. The fact that this exercise in logic was probably written by an undergraduate student shows that a new generation was rebelling against well-established, authoritarian ways of thinking.

Phrased differently, smart, young punks were making ghosts cool again.

This movement grew. About ten years later, students at the same university formed the Cambridge Association for Spiritual Inquiry, a.k.a. the Ghostly Guild, a.k.a. the Ghost

Club. Noted briefly in Chapter Four's section on paranormal investigation teams, this group of enterprising students left behind precious few records of their activities. We have a circular announcing their intentions, though. Here, we read that the group recognized that both believers and unbelievers had "a common interest in wishing cases of supposed 'supernatural' agency to be thoroughly shifted." The problem of such a project is in selecting "a sufficient number of clear and well-attested cases" from those that are "purely fictitious" and the many more that are "a mixture of truth and falsehood." It wouldn't be easy to achieve, but the goal was to establish "an extensive collection of authenticated cases of supposed 'supernatural' agency." Basically, the group wanted to establish a body of reliable evidence on the topic.

Interestingly, the students weren't sure what would be done with that body of evidence. This "must be a subject for future consideration," explains the circular. First things first. Rather than say if evidence would be sought to support or refute the reality of ghosts, the framers of this manifesto proceed to outline how the evidence will be categorized, from angels and specters to presentiments and physical manifestations. Exactly how far the project progressed in gathering data isn't known—one source says the members "collected two thousand cases of apparitions" while another says the project "does not seem to have obtained very satisfactory results; at all events, its originators did not go beyond the preliminary inquiry."[17] Regardless of the results, the circular shows the students were doing what Colton advocated: know all the facts before formulating theories.

Those Cambridge students weren't alone in wanting to provide scholars with a collection of cases challenging pervasive assumptions about ghosts. At about the same time, the same goal was being pursued by Catherine Crowe, who had assembled a casebook of prophetic dreams, doppelgangers, apparitions, haunted houses, poltergeists, and more. In *The Night Side of Nature* (1848), Crowe explains, "The contemptuous sceptism of the last age is yielding to a more humble spirit of inquiry." Though a believer herself, she reiterated Colton's prescription to patiently assemble facts before drawing conclusions. To her, paranormal investigation meant "the slow, modest, painstaking examination that is content to wait upon nature and humbly follow out her disclosures, however opposed to preconceived theories or mortifying to human pride." The phrase "to wait on *nature*" reveals Crowe's understanding of spectral and related phenomena: they were *natural* issues and, therefore, a subject for scientists. She flatly states that, "in undertaking to treat of the phenomena in question, I do not propose to consider them supernatural; on the contrary, I am persuaded that the time will come when they will be reduced strictly within the bounds of science."[18] Much as ΨYXH refutes the argument that ghosts contradict natural laws by nudging readers to think of them as being a part of those laws, Crowe drops the *super* from *supernatural*.

In terms of a body of evidence for scientific scrutiny, however, Crowe probably did more to *inspire* the hunt for such evidence than to supply it. One early reviewer of *Night Side* points out that there was a need for a "collection of ghost stories, second-sight tales, fulfilled dreams, and other incidents of a supernatural kind." This ideal book should

> accurately trace up every tale to its original source, so that the reader should have distinctly before him the exact authorities upon which the account rests; since very often, if they were thoroughly sifted, they would from their time or character be found to be totally unworthy of credit, or not possessing the *kind* of credit that would be requisite to establish an improbable natural fact, much more a supernatural story.

Night Side is weak in this regard, says the reviewer. Crowe "frequently omits to quote any authority; and when she does quote, her references are mostly vague, not specifying the book, but merely the writer's name." While *Night Side* lacks careful documentation of its sources, its stories succeed in providing readers with "the true spectral thrill."[19] In this reviewer's opinion, then, the book appeals more to readers seeking spooky excitement rather than verifiable evidence of paranormal activity.

However, the popular appeal of the book proved to be its strength, and by targeting a wide readership, Crowe very likely had a profound effect on reshaping general views. Hardly a decade had passed since its debut when Crowe's ghostly guidebook was being referenced in horror fiction and named as inspiration for poetry. In the 1890s, when a reader sought a collection of ghost stories, Crowe's was still being recommended as the "most famous one." In the early 1900s, in a volume titled *Best Books on Spirit Phenomena, 1847-1925,* Henrietta Lovi places Crowe's book first in her chapter titled "Books to Sit Up All Night to Read." Lovi points out that *Night Side* has been "in demand through edition after edition" and it leaves "the reader breathless as one item follows another—each seemingly more remarkable than its predecessor."[20] The wisest Victorian ghost hunters surely had two copies of Crowe's work: one available for lending and the other saved for personal use.

Okay, it's safer to say the wisest Victorian ghost hunters would have known about *Night Side*. Still, Crowe helped change perceptions of the barriers to the otherworld. In doing so, she made room for psychical research, that late-Victorian form of paranormal investigation especially aimed at séances, clairvoyance, mesmerism, and haunted houses. Lovi points out that, "to so earnest a student and author as Mrs. Crowe, psychical science of the present time is indebted" (by which she meant the mid-1920s). The historian then turns to the founders of that weird science, mentioning physicist William F. Barrett, psychologists William James and James H. Hyslop, and botanist Edward

T. Bennett.[21] These scientists risked their professional reputations by doing psychical research, and they might not have done so if intellectual attitudes hadn't been challenged by some Cambridge students and by Crowe.

Furthermore, these scientists at the end of the century shared the tireless data-gathering methodology that Colton had suggested at the start of it. We can see this in "First Report of the Committee on Haunted Houses," published by the Society for Psychical Research when this organization was in its first year of existence. The committee members agreed to start by assembling "a systematic collection, from trustworthy sources, of evidence bearing on the subject of our researches." If possible, the members would record testimony in person, and if not, they would "conduct a cross-examination by letter." Preferring fresh and firsthand testimony, the committee's criteria for valid data included "some independent evidence to corroborate it." This could mean having *additional* witnesses. It might also involve something unknown to the witness at the time of the encounter being relevant to the case history. For example, the witness was unaware that the night of the encounter, it turns out, was the anniversary of a murder in the same room.

The report then illustrates the committee's methods by relating four investigations. The first three fail to meet the criteria for valid evidence. One involves a painter who— though he could sketch an apparition he saw several times— was alone in witnessing it. The next was disregarded for being too clouded in hearsay and memory, and another for the inability to contact alleged corroborating witnesses. A fourth case shows more promise. Firsthand testimony. Three witnesses. Visual and audible manifestations. A person designated "Miss A—" had died tragically in the house, and it was assumed that the spirit was hers. One witness says the phantom was "friendly toward us, but quite unconnected with our concerns. . . . She never came to warn us, nor to communicate with us." The committee reporter then explains that "any piece of the evidence standing by itself might be ingeniously explained away," but "when the various bits of testimony are put side by side," the case was a strong one.

Interrogating witnesses and assessing the reliability of that testimonial evidence were longstanding elements of ghost hunting, at least as old as Glanvill's investigation of the Mompesson haunting. But what about nocturnal surveillance, which was far older? The Committee report ends by showing the difficulties in this, starting with the slim chance "that any result will be obtained by a single night's experiment" and ending with reluctance of homeowners to openly admit their house is haunted.[22] It would be slow going for these very serious ghost hunters.

The following year, things had stayed about the same. Still with "no very startling theory to propound," the committee continued to focus on "collecting and sifting evidence." Conducting nocturnal surveillance remained fraught with problems, and the reporter says that "we would beg any of our members or friends who are so fortunate as to inhabit haunted houses, to afford us, if possible, some opportunity for investigation."[23] This request for assistance shows the committee's determination—along with a touch of desperation.

As the years progressed, the Society *did* get some opportunities to conduct onsite investigations. Here, too, we see admirable patience. After applying the usual stringent criteria to reports of a supposedly haunted house identified as B— Lodge, the Society rented the place in 1885 and had someone living there from the end of March to the end of September. Other members of the Society visited and "about 50 persons in all appear to have slept in the house during the six months." Footsteps were heard, but it was "inferred that someone from the village had concealed himself in the house with the object of playing the ghost." Earlier reports of strange noises in the house were traced to ordinary noises made outside on a nearby street. What had been reported as "some peculiar stains on the floor of an upper room" proved to be nothing more than paint.[24] Disappointing, yes, but debunking is often a part of the job.

If patience is key to good ghost hunting, imagine conducting surveillance for over thirteen months! That's what Laura and George Smith did. The Society rented a house said to be haunted by moans, footsteps, the spectral face and figure of a melancholy woman, and more. The Smiths occupied the house from August of 1888 to September of 1889. During that time, they hosted 39 guest investigators. George reported, "In one or two cases, these visitors heard noises during the night which they could not quite account for; but in most instances the sounds were so trivial that little importance was attached to them." The Smiths themselves never *saw* anything strange, but they did *hear* "a few odd noises." Probably the most intriguing involved a guitar that hung on the wall of a sitting room. George had just gone to bed, leaving Laura in that room to say her nightly prayers by the warm fire. The husband says:

> In the midst of the quietness which ensued I suddenly heard the guitar play—*pung, pang, ping*—*pung, pang, ping*—here my wife called out in a loud, awe-struck whisper, "Did you hear that?" whilst even as she spoke a third *pung, pang, ping* sounded clearly through the rooms. I immediately sprang out of bed and rushed in to her, finding her kneeling on the hearthrug by an armchair, staring with astonishment at the guitar on the wall.

The guitar remained silent at that point. However, a moment *before* the pung-pang-pinging, Laura had heard "a noise like someone sweeping their hand over the wallpaper." When the strings were sounding, she had presence of mind to observe that nothing was near the instrument and that "it made no perceptible movement."[25] Although this and the few additional mysterious sounds are certainly interesting, one might wonder if the many months the Smiths invested was worth the evidence they were collecting.

The Society thought so. It was amassing enough data for some of its members to sketch fascinating new theories about why human history is so rich in ghostly encounters. In fact, Smith's report on his 13-month investigation is part of Frank Podmore's article laying out a myriad of cases to support a bold theory. He disagrees with the traditional idea that ghosts are "spirits of deceased persons, actually walking this earth in quasi-material form." He also disagrees with a much newer theory that ghosts "are essentially hallucinatory," but "the hallucinations are in some sense due to the agency of a deceased person, that they are possibly a reflection of his uneasy dream; or . . . that they represent in some way the fragmentary thoughts of a decaying personality." This last idea seems to depend on thought-transference between the living and dead, and Podmore wonders if we can remove the telepathic dead altogether. He'd rather explore the possibility that ghosts are hallucinations shared telepathically between people still living. It's mind-bending stuff (which he makes clearer in a book titled *Telepathic Hallucinations: The New View of Ghosts),* and Podmore knew he was just playing with hypotheses and hunches. He still valued meticulously gathering data over drawing any grand conclusions, as seen at the article's end, where he says that—while there's not enough evidence "to prove *post-mortem* agency"—neither is "such agency disproved." For now, "the elaboration of theories should be subordinated to the collection and verification of evidence."[26] Indeed, speculation—even sketchy speculation—might open new avenues to finding evidence.

Colton certainly would have approved.

Lessons of Ghost Hunting's Long History

I am not suggesting that Colton had any significant, *direct* influence on the Victorian call for prioritizing data collecting over theorizing. Still, any ghost hunter who knew about the clergyman's refusal to jump to conclusions (and who took him at his word) could have seen him as an exemplar, a ghost hunter worthy of admiration and emulation. When the urge to solve the mystery rises—but the evidence just isn't enough—a ghost hunter can find strength by whispering: "Remember Colton." That's as true for the Victorians as for paranormal investigators today.

Much the same can be said about all of the ghost hunters discussed in this book. Even as a legend—and maybe because of it—Athenodorus serves as a model of approaching a spooky site with calm reserve, letting curiosity lead to a truth that others have missed. Remember Athenodorus. Yet don't forget Parson Dodge. Sometimes there's good reason to be afraid.

And remember that, sometimes, debunking leads to the truth that others have missed. Deshoulières's legend reminds us of this, as does the factual history of Aldrich, Johnson, and their team members who investigated the Cock Lane case. On the other hand, Parson Ruddle illustrates how *too much* skepticism can also block the discovery of what's truly happening. Remember that believing or disbelieving in ghosts can be a matter of balance instead of extremes.

When a ghost hunt seems to go wrong—the batteries of the night-vision goggles are dead and the EVP recorder is glitching—there might be some comfort in recalling Francis Smith on Black Lion Lane, Hammersmith. Things could go worse. A *lot* worse. This might be where the mysterious but poetic Mr. Nolan comes in to urge us to be prepared to use an otherwise unproductive ghost hunt to accomplish something else. There's nothing wrong with multitasking.

Jervis, Bolton, and Luttrell at Hinton Ampner show

how, at times, a haunting *can't* be sorted out at all. Ghosts might not be lingering for any discernable purpose. Colton's patient perseverance is commendable, but it's good to know when to call it quits and move to the next haunted hotspot, too.

These founders of ghost hunting can serve as inspiration or as warning. Whether ghosts are real is still debated, but most people would agree that *spirits* persist for centuries. And the spirits of these ghost hunters, who embarked on their quests before the Victorians, continue to walk among us long after them.

---

[1] Review of *Hypocrisy: A Satire in Three Books,* by C. Colton, *British Critic* 42 (October 1813) p. 331. Richard Alfred Davenport, *Sketches of Imposture, Deception, and Credulity* (Thomas Tegg and Son, 1837) p. 153. "A Queer Parson," *Belgravia* 51 (August 1883) p. 187. John H. Ingram, *The Haunted Homes and Family Traditions of Great Britain,* Second Series (W.H. Allen & Co., 1884) p. 226.

[2] J.D., "Tale of Mystery—the Following Curious Narrative Has Been Authenticated to Us by a Correspondent," *Morning Chronicle,* August 2, 1810, p. 3.

[3] The original letter was adapted to articles in the *Sun,* August 2, 1810, p. 3; *St. James's Chronicle,* August 4, 1810, p. 3; and the *Examiner,* August 5, 1810, p. 7. Marriott's intent to debunk is announced in *Taunton Courier,* August 16, 1810, issue p. 8/volume p. 800.

[4] "Sampford Ghost," *Taunton Chronicle,* August 23, 1810, issue p. 6/volume p. 806.

[5] "The Sampford Ghost," *Examiner,* August 26, 1810, pp. 15-16. On Marriott's association with the Hunt brothers, see his obituary in the *Examiner,* February 18, 1865, p. 108.

[6] Assertions #1 through #3 and the comparison of the manifestations to Satanic witchcraft are made in "Sampford Ghost," *Taunton Courier,* September 13, 1810, issue p. 8/ volume p. 832; #4 and #5 in "Sampford Ghost," *Taunton Courier,* August 30, 1810, issue p. 5/volume p. 813; and #6 through #10 and the concluding remarks in "Sampford Ghost," *Taunton Courier,* September 20, 1810, issue p. 6/ volume p. 838. That Moon professionally performed "sleight-of-hand, and conjuring, etc." is confirmed in "Sampford Ghost," *London Chronicle,* October 16-17, 1810, p. 372.

⁷ C. Colton, *Sampford Ghost: A Plain and Authentic Narrative,* (Printed by T. Smith, 1910) pp. 4, 9.

⁸ "Sampford Ghost," *Tautonton Courier,* September 20, 1818, issue p. 6/volume p. 838. C. Colton, *Sampford Ghost: A Plain and Authentic Narrative,* pp. 14-17.

⁹ One clue that Colton was writing *A Plain and Authentic Narrative* during the weeks that Marriott's articles were appearing is in a footnote. He mentions that Chave provided him some updated information, opening his sentence this way: "This morning, September 25ᵗʰ. . . ." This is five days after the last article was published. Marriott then reprinted those articles in *Sampford Ghost!!! A Full Account of the Conspiracy at Sampford Peverell* (Printed for I. Norris, 1810).

¹⁰ In C. Colton, *Sampford Ghost: Stubborn Facts Against Vague Assertions* (Printed by T. Smith, 1810), Talley's and Chave's occupancy of the house is addressed on pp. 5-7, the mopstick on p. 11, and the battens and ceiling marks on pp. 13-14. In the same source, Dodge's innocence is discussed on p. 9, Taylor's on p. 15, and Case's on p. 7.

¹¹ Colton, *Sampford Ghost: Stubborn Facts Against Vague Assertions,* p. 27. C. Colton, *Hypocrisy: A Satire in Three Books,* vol. 1 (Printed by T. Smith, 1812) p. 293.

¹² Frederick John Snell, *The Chronicles of Twyford* (Gregory, Son & Tozer, 1892) p. 235.

¹³ S. Baring-Gould, *Devonshire Characters and Strange Events* (John Lane, 1908) pp. 290-291. The Stockwell hoax is discussed in Charles Mackay, *Memoirs of Popular Delusions and the Madness of Crowds,* vol. 2 (Office of the National Illustrated Library, 1852) pp. 234-235.

¹⁴ Charles G. Harper, *Haunted Houses: Tales of the Supernatural* (Chapman & Hall, 1907) pp. 122, 128-129.

¹⁵ "To Our Readers," *Cambridge University Magazine,* 1.2 (May 1839) p. 80.

¹⁶ ΨΥΧΗ, "A Chapter on Ghosts," *Cambridge University Magazine* 1.2 (May 1839) pp. 145-149.

¹⁷ The circular is reprinted as "Appendix: Note A" in Robert Dale Owen's *Footfalls on the Boundary of Another World* (J.B. Lippincott, 1860) pp. 513-515. The claim that two thousand cases were gathered is mentioned in Epes Sargent's *Planchett; or, The Despair of Science* (Roberts Brothers, 1869) p. 203. (Sargent cites Owen as his source, but I haven't found that figure mentioned in *Footfalls.*) The more modest estimate is in G.W. Prothero's *A Memoir of Henry Bradshaw* (Kegan Paul, Trench & Co., 1888) p. 26.

[18] Catherine Crowe, *The Night Side of Nature; Or, Ghosts and Ghost Seers,* vol. 1 (T.C. Newby, 1848) pp. 4-5, 17.

[19] "Mrs. Crowe's Night-Side of Nature," *Spectator* 21 (January 29, 1848) pp. 110-111.

[20] In horror fiction, *Night Side* is mentioned in Fitz-James O'Brien's "What Was It?" *Harper's* 18 (March 1859) p. 505, and it's cited as inspiration in Algayer Hay Hill's "Lines After Reading Mrs. Crowe's 'Night-side of Nature,'" *Footprints of Life and Other Poems* (H. Davies, 1857) p. 41. The "most famous" recommendation is in "The Literary Querist," *Book Buyer* 10 (October 1893) p. 381. Henrietta Lovi, *Best Books on Spirit Phenomena, 1847-1925* (R.G. Badger, 1925) p. 79. The publishing history of Crowe's *The Night Side of Nature* is impressive. After the original edition indicated in footnote 18, it was republished in the UK by G. Routlege in 1857, 1866, and 1882. In the US, it was published by J.S. Redfield in 1850 and 1853, by W.J. Widdleton in 1868, and by Henry T. Coates in 1901. There are probably other editions out there, too.

[21] Lovi, pp. 13-18.

[22] "First Report of the Committee on Haunted Houses," *Proceedings of the Society for Psychical Research* 1 (December 9, 1882) pp. 101-115.

[23] "Second Report of the Committee on Haunted Houses," *Proceedings of the Society for Psychical Research* 2 (Mar. 28, 1884) pp. 137-138.

[24] Frank Podmore, "An Account of Some Abnormal Phenomena Alleged to Have Occurred at B— Lodge, W—," *Journal of the Society for Psychical Research* 2 (February 1886) pp. 205-207.

[25] The Brighton case, designated G. 187, is reported in Frank Podmore's "Phantasms of the Dead from Another Point of View," *Proceedings of the Society for Psychical Research* 6 (November 29, 1889) pp. 255-269. This article is followed by an Appendix on pp. 309-313, which is mostly made up of George Smith's report. The investigator is identified as "X.Y." there, but confirmation that it was Smith is provided by his signed letter regarding the case, reprinted in "The Journalist at Large in Psychical Research," *Journal of the Society for Psychical Research* 12 (April 1905) p. 68.

[26] "Phantasms of the Dead from Another Point of View," p. 229, 308. The book enlarging on Podmore's provocative theory is *Telepathic Hallucinations: The New View of Ghosts* (Frederick A. Stokes, 1910).

APPENDIX:
FRANCIS GROSE ON GHOSTLORE

Francis Grose (1731-1791) was a talented visual artist. One of his drawings can be seen on the cover of this book. He was also an accomplished antiquarian, an old term for a historian with a focus on physical artifacts, be they ruinous castles, peeling oil portraits, or yellowing church records. Grose was equally interested in "artifacts" embedded in the language and customs—be they old-fashioned terms and slang, or traditional sayings and beliefs—found in England's rural areas. This makes him a lexicographer, a linguist, and a folklorist, too. [1]

Regarding these latter interests, Grose organized his findings into a book titled A Provincial Glossary, with a Collection of Local Proverbs and Popular Superstitions *(1787). It includes a good discussion of ghostlore, revealing how people understood specters fifty years before the Victorian era began. At times, Grose gives the impression that he finds these beliefs enchanting—but also rather silly. Although there's an air of superiority over people "in former times," it's mixed with an awareness that, given time, people probably will be looking back at "now" with a very similar attitude. I like to think Grose recorded these folk beliefs to*

---

[1] The illustration is from *The Antiquities of Scotland,* vol. 2 (Printed for Hooper and Wigstead, 1797) between pp. 66-67. Regarding Grose's status as a founding folklorist, see Venetia Newall, "Francis Grose, Folklore's Forerunner," *RSA Journal* 140.5426 (Feb. 1992) pp. 187-192.

capture where we've been because knowing that encourages readers to consider where we're headed.

The following reproduces the opening paragraphs of his introduction to a section titled "Superstitions" and the entirety of a subsection titled "A Ghost." [2]

— *Tim Prasil*

---

[2] The discussion presented here can be found in Francis Grose, *A Provincial Glossary, with a Collection of Local Proverbs, and Popular Superstitions* (Printed for S. Hooper, 1787) pp. 1-4, 6-17 of the "Superstitions" section.

It will scarcely be conceived how great a number of superstitious notions and practices are still remaining and prevalent in different parts of these kingdoms, many of which are still used and alluded to even in and about the metropolis; and every person, however carefully educated, will, upon examination, find that he has somehow or other imbibed and stored up in his memory a much greater number of these rules and maxims than he could at first have imagined.

To account for this, we need only turn our recollection towards what passed in our childhood, and reflect on the avidity and pleasure with which we listened to stories of ghosts, witches, and fairies, told us by our maids and nurses. And even among those whose parents had the good sense to prohibit such relations, there is scarce one in a thousand but may remember to have heard, from some maiden aunt or antiquated cousin, the various omens that have announced the approaching deaths of different branches of the family; a copious catalogue of things lucky and unlucky; a variety of charms to cure warts, the cramp, and toothache; preventatives against the nightmare; with observations relative to sympathy, denoted by shiverings, burning of the cheeks, and itchings of the eyes and elbows. The effects of ideas of this kind are not easily got the better of, and the ideas themselves rarely, if ever, forgotten.

In former times, these notions were so prevalent that it was deemed little less than atheism to doubt them, and in many instances, the terrors caused by them embittered the lives of a great number of persons of all ages, by degrees almost shutting them out of their own houses and deterring them from going from one village to another after sunset. The room in which the head of a family had died was for a long time untenanted, particularly if they died without a will or were supposed to have entertained any particular religious opinions. But if any disconsolate old maiden or love-crossed bachelor happened to dispatch themselves in their garters,[1] the room where the deed was perpetrated was rendered forever after uninhabitable and, not unfrequently, was nailed up. If a drunken farmer, returning from market, fell from Old Dobbin[2] and broke his neck—or a carter, under the same predicament, tumbled from his cart or wagon, and was killed by it—that spot was ever after haunted and impassable. In short, there was scarcely a bylane or crossway but had its ghost, who appeared in the shape of a headless cow or horse or, clothed all in white, glared with its saucer eyes over a gate or stile.

Ghosts of superior rank, when they appeared abroad, rode in coaches drawn by six headless horses and driven by a headless coachman and postilions. Almost every ancient manor house was haunted by some one, at least, of its former masters or mistresses, where, besides diverse other noises, that of telling money was distinctly heard. As for the churchyards, the number of ghosts that walked there, according to the village computation, almost equalled the living parishioners. To pass them at night was an achievement not to be attempted by anyone in the parish, the sextons excepted, who perhaps being particularly privileged, to make use of the common expression, never saw anything worse than themselves. . . .

A ghost is supposed to be the spirit of a person deceased, who is either commissioned to return for some especial errand—such as the discovery of a murder or to procure restitution of lands or money unjustly withheld from an orphan or widow—or, having committed some injustice

---

[1] This means they committed suicide.

[2] Dobbin refers to a horse, especially one that moves slowly and works on a farm.

whilst living, cannot rest till that is redressed. Sometimes, the occasion of spirits revisiting this world is to inform their heir in what secret place or private drawer in an old trunk they had hidden the title deeds of the estate or where, in troublesome times, they buried their money or plate.[3] Some ghosts of murdered persons, whose bodies have been secretly buried, cannot be at ease till their bones have been taken up and deposited in consecrated ground with all the rites of Christian burial. This idea is the remains of a very old piece of heathen superstition: the Ancients believed that Charon was not permitted to ferry over the ghosts of unburied persons, but that they wandered up and down the banks of the river Styx for a hundred years, after which they were admitted to a passage. This is mentioned by Virgil:

Hæc omnis quam cernis, inops inhumataque turba est:
Portitor ille, Charon; hi quos vehit unda, sepulti.
Nec ripas datur horrendas, nec rauca fluenta,
Transportare prius quam sedibus ossa quièrunt,
Centum errant annos, volitantque hæc littora circum:
Tum, demum admissi, stagna exoptata revisunt.[4]

---

[3] Plate refers to diningware made of valuable metal, such as silver.

[4] These are lines 325-330 in Book 6 of Virgil's *Aeneid.* A 1753 edition offers this translation:

>Those, who neglected on the strand remain,
>Are all a wretched, poor, unburied train.
>Charon is he, who o'er the flood presides;
>And those interr'd, who cross the Stygian tides.
>No mortal pass the hoarse-resounding wave,
>But those who slumber in a peaceful grave.
>Thus, till a hundred years have roll'd away,
>Around these shores the plaintive spectres stray.
>That mighty term expir'd, their wanderings pass,
>They reach the long expected shore at last.

The Works of Virgil, in Latin and English, translated by Christopher Pitt, vol. 3 (Printed for R. Dodsley, 1753) p. 205.

Sometimes ghosts appear in consequence of an agreement made, whilst living, with some particular friend, that he who first died should appear to the survivor.

Glanvill tells us of the ghost of a person who had lived but a disorderly kind of life, for which it was condemned to wander up and down the earth, in the company of evil spirits, till the Day of Judgment.[5]

In most of the relations of ghosts, they are supposed to be mere aerial beings, without substance, and that they can pass through walls and other solid bodies at pleasure. A particular instance of this is given in Relation 27 in Glanvill's collection, where one David Hunter, neatherd[6] to the Bishop of Down and Connor, was for a long time haunted by the apparition of an old woman. He was, by a secret impulse, obliged to follow this ghost whenever she appeared, which he says he did for a considerable time, even if in bed with his wife. Because his wife could not hold him in his bed, she would go, too, and walk after him till day, though she saw nothing. His little dog was so well acquainted with the apparition that he would follow it as well as his master. If a tree stood in her walk, he observed her always to go through it. Notwithstanding this seeming immateriality, this very ghost was not without some substance, for, having performed her errand, she desired Hunter to lift her from the ground. In the doing of which, he says, she felt just like a bag of feathers.

We sometimes also read of ghosts striking violent blows, and that, if not made way for, they overturn all

---

[5] This refers to Relation 18 of Joseph Glanvill's *Sadducismus Triumphatus; Or, Full and Plain Evidence Concerning Witches and Apparitions* (Printed for J. Colling, 1681) pp. 245-249. Grose's subsequent references refer to this work. (This is the same Glanvill as discussed in Chapter Three of this book.)

[6] A neatherd cares for cows.

impediments, like a furious whirlwind. Glanvill mentions an instance of this, in Relation 17, of a Dutch lieutenant, who had the faculty of seeing ghosts and who, being prevented from making way for one, which he mentioned to some friends as coming towards them, was with his companions violently thrown down and sorely bruised. We further learn, by Relation 16, that the hand of a ghost is "as cold as a clod."

The usual time at which ghosts make their appearance is midnight, and seldom before it is dark, though some audacious spirits have been said to appear even by daylight. But of this, there are few instances, and those mostly ghosts who have been laid, perhaps in the Red Sea (of which more hereafter) and whose times of confinement were expired. These, like felons confined to the lighters,[7] are said to return more troublesome and daring than before.

No ghosts can appear on Christmas Eve—this Shakespeare has put into the mouth of one of his characters in *Hamlet*.[8]

Ghosts commonly appear in the same dress they usually wore whilst living. They are sometimes clothed all in white, but that is chiefly the churchyard ghosts, who have no particular business, but seem to appear *pro bono publico*[9] or to scare drunken rustics from tumbling over their graves.

I cannot learn if ghosts carry tapers in their hands, as

---

[7] Lighters were prison ships, also called ballast lighters or prison hulks. In 1788, Sarah Trimmer wrote: "Onboard the ballast-lighter criminals are condemned to wear a heavy chain—to be driven about like horses—to work very hard without wages, and to be under continual restraint—and to be exposed to the eye of the world as *villains.*" *The Sunday-School Catechist* (Printed by T. Benley, 1788) p. 166.

[8] In the Bard's famous play, Marcellus tells Horatio: "Some say that ever 'gainst that season comes / Wherein our Savior's birth is celebrated, / . . . no spirit dares stirs abroad." (1.1.173-176).

[9] *Pro bono publico* is a Latin phrase describing unpaid work done for the public good.

they are sometimes depicted, though the room in which they appear, if without fire or candle, is frequently said to be as light as day. Dragging chains is not the fashion of English ghosts. Chains and black vestments are chiefly the accouterments of foreign spectres, seen in arbitrary governments— dead or alive, English spirits are free. One instance, however, of an English ghost dressed in black is found in the celebrated ballad of William and Margaret, in the following lines:

> And clay-cold was her lily hand,
> That held her sable shroud.[10]

This, however, may be considered as a poetical licence, used in all likelihood for the sake of the opposition of lily to sable.

If, during the time of an apparition, there is a lighted candle in the room, it will burn extremely blue. This is so universally acknowledged that many eminent philosophers have busied themselves in accounting for it without once doubting the truth of the fact. Dogs, too, have the faculty of seeing spirits—as instanced in David Hunter's relation, above quoted—but in that case, they usually show signs of terror by whining and creeping to their master for protection. It is generally supposed that they often see things of this nature when their owner cannot, there being some persons, particularly those born on a Christmas Eve, who cannot see spirits.

The coming of a spirit is announced sometime before its

---

[10] This comes from David Mallet's poem "William and Margaret," as shown in the "The Poems of David Mallet, Esq." section of *The Works of the English Poets,* vol. 53 (Printed by J. Riverton, 1779) p.153. Grose might have known it from *The Tea-Table Miscellany: A Collection of Choice Songs , Scots and English,* edited by Allan Ramsay, 18th ed. (Printed by J. MacNair, 1782) p. 312. There, it's presented anonymously and as "An old ballad."

appearance by a variety of loud and dreadful noises, sometimes rattling in the old hall like a coach and six, and rumbling up and down the staircase like the trundling of bowls or cannon balls. At length, the door flies open, and the spectre stalks slowly up to the bed's foot and, opening the curtains, looks steadfastly at the person in bed by whom it is seen. A ghost is very rarely visible to more than one person, although there are several in company. It is here necessary to observe that it has been universally found, by experience as well as affirmed by diverse apparitions themselves, that a ghost has not the power to speak till it has been first spoken to. Notwithstanding the urgency of the business on which it may come, everything must stand still till the person visited can find sufficient courage to speak to it, an event that sometimes does not take place for many years. It has not been found that female ghosts are more loquacious than those of the male sex, both being equally restrained by this law.

The mode of addressing a ghost is by commanding it, in the name of the Three Persons of the Trinity, to tell you who it is and what is its business. It may be necessary to repeat this three times. Afterward, it will, in a low and hollow voice, declare its satisfaction at being spoken to and desire the party addressing it not to be afraid, for it will do him no harm. This being premised, it commonly enters into its narrative, which being completed and its request or commands given with injunctions that they be immediately executed, it vanishes away, frequently in a flash of light. Some ghosts, upon disappearing, have been so considerate as to desire the party to whom they appeared to shut their eyes. Sometimes, its departure is attended with delightful music. During the narration of its business, a ghost must by no means be interrupted by questions of any kind—doing so is extremely dangerous. If any doubts arise, they must be stated *after* the spirit has done its tale. Questions respecting its state or the state of any of their former acquaintances, are offensive and not often answered. Perhaps, spirits are restrained from divulging the secrets of their prison house.

Occasionally, spirits will even condescend to talk on common occurrences, as is instanced by Glanvill, in the apparition of Major George Sydenham to Captain William Dyke, Relation 10, wherein the Major reproved the Captain for suffering a sword he had given him to grow rusty. He said, "Captain, Captain, this sword did not use to be kept after this manner when it was mine." This attention to the state of arms was a remnant of the Major's professional duty when living.

It is somewhat remarkable that ghosts do not go about their business like the persons of this world. In cases of murder, a ghost—instead of going to the next justice of the peace and laying its information, or to the nearest relation of the person murdered—appears to some poor labourer who knows none of the parties, draws the curtains of some decrepit nurse or almswoman, or hovers about the place where his body is deposited. The same circuitous mode is pursued with respect to redressing injured orphans or widows, when it seems as if the shortest and most certain way would be to go to the person guilty of the injustice and haunt him continually till he be terrified into a restitution. Nor are the pointing out lost writings generally managed in a more summary way. The ghost commonly applies to a third person, ignorant of the whole affair and a stranger to all concerned. But it is presumptuous to scrutinize too far into these matters. Ghosts have, undoubtedly, forms and customs peculiar to themselves.

If, after the first appearance, the persons employed neglect or are prevented from performing the message or business committed to their management, the ghost appears continually to them. At first, it exhibits a discontented countenance, next an angry one, and at length a furious appearance, threatening to tear them to pieces if the matter is not forthwith executed. Sometimes, it terrifies them, as in

Glanvill's Relation 26, by appearing in many formidable shapes and occasionally even striking them a violent blow. Of blows given by ghosts there are many instances, and some wherein they have been followed with an incurable lameness.

It should have been observed that ghosts, in delivering their commissions, in order to ensure belief, communicate to the persons employed some secret, known only to the parties concerned and themselves, the relation of which always produces the effect intended. The business being completed, ghosts appear with a cheerful countenance, saying they shall now be at rest and will never more disturb anyone. Thanking their agents by way of reward, the ghosts communicate something relative to them, which they will never reveal.

Sometimes, ghosts appear and disturb a house without deigning to give any reason for so doing. With these, the shortest and only way is to exorcise and eject them or, as the vulgar term is, lay them.[11]

For this purpose there must be two or three clergymen, and the ceremony must be performed in Latin, a language that strikes the most audacious ghost with terror. A ghost may be laid for any term less than an hundred years, and in any place or body, full or empty, as a solid oak; the pommel of a sword; a barrel of beer, if a yeoman or simple gentleman; or a pipe of wine, if an esquire or a justice. But of all places the most common—and what a ghost least likes—is the Red Sea. It is related, in many instances, that ghosts have most earnestly besought the exorcists not to confine them in that place. It is nevertheless considered as an indisputable fact that there are an infinite number laid there, perhaps from its being a safer prison than any other nearer at hand. Neither history nor tradition gives us any instance of ghosts escaping

---

[11] Here, vulgar means commonplace rather than offensive.

or returning from this kind of transportation before their time.[12]

---

[12] In keeping with Grose's previous parallels between ghosts and prisoners, transportation refers to being punished via exile. English convicts, for example, were often transported to Australia. In her effort to foster good behavior, Sarah Trimmer continues her lesson mentioned in footnote 7: "If working in the ballast lighters is so bad, what must it be to be cast out of one's native land as unfit to live among honest people, and transported to a foreign country!—to bid adieu perhaps forever to Old England!—to take a sorrowful and most likely a last farewell of parents, wife, children, and friends!" From there, her description of the experience grows bleaker and bleaker. Trimmer, p.167. Compared to this, I'd say it's far less terrifying and traumatic to raise a kid on ghost stories.

INDEX

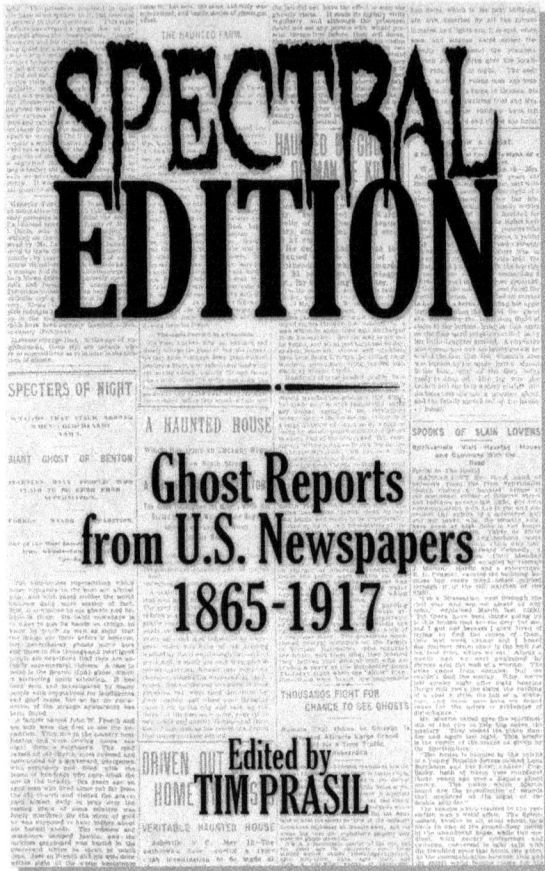